A Teacher's Guide
to
Stephen Wylen's

The Book of the
Jewish Year

Ellen Greenspan

UAHC Press
New York

Contents

Introduction

The Book of the Jewish Year and Its Teacher's Guide

About the Textbook and Its Organization

The Book of the Jewish Year is a textbook about the Jewish holiday cycle for students in the intermediate grades. Most students will come to this textbook with some prior knowledge of the holidays from previous religious school experiences and/or family observance. The book reinforces basic information about each holiday and its rituals. In addition, it introduces students to Jewish folklore, Jewish texts, and the laws and customs of each holiday. It also shows how the cycle of the Jewish year flows and how the Jewish calendar helps us keep track of the year and the things we do each season.

Students will explore traditional holiday rituals and learn how different Jews choose to observe each holiday. The textbook helps students reflect on their own holiday experiences and discover ways in which they can enrich their celebrations.

All the chapters of the textbook are structured in the same way and include the same basic elements. Each chapter begins with a quote about the holy day or festival. After a brief introductory paragraph, each chapter continues with a **Story** from a variety of Jewish sources, both ancient and modern. Next comes a section called **Mitzvot and Minhagim**, which outlines the basic laws and customs of each holy day. This is followed by a **Text Study** section, which introduces students to relevant texts from a variety of classic Jewish sources. The next section, which contains a discussion of each **Holiday Experience**, includes blessings, explanations of traditional observances, and ways in which observances may differ among different Jewish communities. Many chapters also feature a section called **Jewish Family Album**, which tells about the holiday experiences of one particular family. The **Summary** section of each chapter recaps its essential facts and themes.

In addition, two sections appear in some chapters and not in others. One is the **Focus** section, which explores one or two aspects of the holiday in greater depth. The other is **Times and Places**, which presents the historical origins of some aspect of the festival being studied. The book also features bright pictures and graphics illustrating each holiday.

1

About the Teacher's Guide

A Teacher's Guide to the Book of the Jewish Year will help you effectively present each chapter of the textbook to your students. The guide suggests ways to use the textbook and includes discussion questions and activities. It also offers a variety of suggestions that will enable you to supplement the material in the text, helping you enrich your students' understanding of the holidays. The lessons presented here are merely suggestions to help you get started. Teachers are encouraged to bring their own ideas and creativity to the use of this textbook, as well as expand upon the material found in this teacher's guide.

How the Teacher's Guide Is Organized

The chapters in the teacher's guide correspond to the chapters in the textbook and are divided into the sections described below. The following guidelines will help you develop one or more lessons for each chapter:

Chapter Summary lists the key points presented in the chapter, providing an overview of its contents.

Instructional Objectives lists several measurable objectives that students should achieve by reading the chapter and participating in the learning activities.

Key Terms highlights and defines significant words used in the chapter.

Learning Activities presents activities and questions that will enable students to better understand the meaning of each holiday and its rituals. Each Learning Activities section starts with a list of **Materials** that students and teachers will need in order to do the activities that follow. Next comes an **Opening** exercise, which introduces students to the holiday and asks them to think about something they already know pertaining to it. The questions and activities that come after the Opening are based on the chapter sections in the textbook. Therefore, every chapter has a **Story Study** and a **Text Study Review** section, which contain questions that can be posed to students. Every chapter also has a section called **Holiday Experience Activities,** which consists of activities that teachers can assign to students. Other sections like **Focus on Focus, Exploring Times and Places,** and **Family Album Focus** include additional activities for teachers to conduct with students. Each Learning Activities section ends with a concluding feature titled **Closure.**

Most chapters also include sections titled **Questions to Think About** or **Something to Think About** and **Journal Entry,** in which students are asked to synthesize the material they have learned in the chapter and express an opinion about it. These two sections are often designed as writing projects and can be done in class or as homework assignments. Many chapters also contain an **Enrichment Activities** section, which includes additional activities that can be used to expand the lesson on the holiday, and a **Resources** section, in which books, recordings, and other material for further study are listed.

Using the Textbook: Overall Strategies

Each lesson is based on a corresponding chapter in the textbook and assumes that students have already read the chapter. Here are some suggestions for ways to use the text effectively:

- Lead the class in reading the chapter aloud, having students take turns reading it, paragraph by paragraph. You may stop the reading at any point to ask questions about the sections. This option enables you to prompt and guide students, as well as to answer students' questions as they arise.

- Assign chapters as homework to be read and completed before the class meets. By doing this, you can then devote class time to focusing on discussions and the various learning and enrichment activities.

- Allot time at the beginning of class for individual silent reading. Follow with discussions and some of the learning and/or enrichment activities.

- Have students read the chapters or portions of them in pairs or small groups. The groups can then work together on the various learning and enrichment activities.

On the Question of Time

Each teacher, in consultation with the director of education, will decide how much time to devote to a holiday. After students have read a chapter, a basic lesson on the holiday it features can be completed in a single, one-hour class period. The more time you have to spend on a holiday, the more you can delve into its rituals, customs, and observances.

Although this book presents the holidays in the order in which they occur in the Jewish calendar, beginning with Rosh Hashanah, the holidays do not have to be taught in that sequence. Often we cannot devote as much time as we would like to the High Holy Days because of the rushed nature of the beginning of the school year, rushed in part because the fall holidays come in such quick succession. Therefore, you might want to consider taking the time to teach these holy days in a thorough manner even after they have passed.

The same applies to Purim and Pesach. Because these holidays occur so close in succession, one of them is usually studied more thoroughly than the other. Either prepare and teach the material about Purim well enough in advance to allow you to allot the time you will need for the class to study Pesach thoroughly, or introduce one of these holidays at another time of the year. For example, instead of teaching all the holidays in the order in which they fall, think about studying the holidays in groups: the Three Pilgrimage Festivals, the High Holy Days, and the Minor Festivals. Finally, although the chapters of *The Book of the Jewish Year* are designed to coincide with the cycle of the year, each one can be taught as an independent unit.

Opening

The lessons that students remember best are those that begin creatively. Start each lesson in a way that grabs students' attention, highlights the main themes of the lesson, introduces the major concepts and vocabulary of the holiday, and relates the holiday to students' lives.

Learning Activities

1. Have students read the chapter, using one of the strategies described above.

2. Pose questions to pique students' curiosity and to elicit their thoughts. Encourage students to ask whatever questions they may have about the content of the chapter.

3. Choose one or more Learning Activities to reinforce the information presented in the text.

4. Use the pictures and illustrations to deepen students' understanding of the holidays. Ask questions that will encourage students to make connections between their newly acquired knowledge and the pictures.

Closure

Don't leave the lesson open-ended even if you are not finished teaching the holiday. Conclude each lesson with a review of the key points and vocabulary. Discuss briefly what students can look forward to the next time you meet.

Chapter One

Jewish Calendar

Chapter Summary

- The Jewish calendar provides the Jewish people with a sense of unity.

- The Jewish calendar tells us when the seasons arrive and when the holy days of the Jewish year fall.

- The celebration of Jewish holidays begins at sundown, which marks the beginning of the Jewish day.

- Jewish holidays fall into one of four categories: *Shalosh Regalim*, the "Three Pilgrimage Festivals"; minor festivals; fast days; and *Yamim Noraim*, the "Days of Awe" or High Holy Days.

- The Jewish calendar is lunar. Each Jewish month begins with the new moon. The first day of each month is called Rosh Chodesh, the "Head of the Month."

Instructional Objectives

Students will be able to:

- Identify the six Jewish holidays that are mentioned in the Torah.

- Describe the four different types of Jewish holidays.

- Explain some of the differences between the Gregorian calendar and the Jewish calendar.

Key Terms

Chag (pl. Chagim)	A festival.
Minhag	A custom; a commonly accepted observance.

Mitzvah	A commandment from God that is based on the teachings in the Torah.
Moadim	Holidays.
Rosh Chodesh	The Head of the Month; the celebration of the new month.
Shalosh Regalim	The Three Pilgrimage Festivals.
Tzom	A fast.
Yamim Noraim	The Days of Awe; the High Holy Days.
Yom chol (pl. Yemei chol)	An ordinary day.
Yom kodesh (pl. Yemei kodesh)	A holy day.

Learning Activities

Materials

Bibles; a combination Jewish/Gregorian calendar for each student; construction paper and other art supplies for making a calendar; a biblical concordance; a perpetual calendar.

Opening

Ask students about the calendars they use. Ask: What type of information do your calendars contain? Does your family have a "master calendar"? What kinds of things are listed on it? (family chores, outings, celebrations, etc.) Do you use a calendar to remind you of upcoming events? Do you or your family use more than one kind of calendar? (Possible answers include: wall calendar, pocket diary, desk calendar, secular calendar, school calendar, Jewish calendar.)

Story Study (pp. 2-3)

1. Ask students the following questions:

   • Why did the people ask Honi to pray? What were they afraid of? (In the days of the ancient Temple, the High Priests offered sacrifices on behalf of the people. Communal prayer as we know it today had not yet been introduced. Instead, High Priests acted as intermediaries between the Israelites and God. Because the people thought that God might not hear or listen to their prayers, they asked Honi to pray. They were afraid that if the rains didn't come, neither would spring because the order of the world was cyclical.)

   • What do you think is the significance of the circle? (The circle signifies the cycle of the seasons. In a sense, the seasons travel in a circle as we move through the year. Circles, which are round, symbolize the cycles of our lives.)

- Do you think that Honi really influenced the changing of the seasons? Explain your answer.

2. At the end of the story, Honi looks up and offers a little prayer of thanks to God. Have students write their own brief prayer thanking God for the cycle of the seasons.

Text Study Review (pp. 4-5)

1. Which six Jewish holidays are mentioned in the Torah? (Shabbat, Pesach, Shavuot, Rosh Hashanah, Yom Kippur, and Sukot)

2. Have students look in a Bible at the source of this text. Tell them to look specifically at Leviticus 23:33-36. Ask: What additional information about Sukot is given? (Sukot also is a "sacred occasion," and no work is permitted on the first day.)

3. Continue by asking students the following questions:

- What do you think the term "sacred occasion" means? (It refers to a day set apart. In Hebrew the word *kodesh*, which we translate as "holy," actually means "set apart." The term is used for a day on which no work is permitted, as well as a holy day that has special observances associated with it.)

- Which three holidays have an agricultural component? (Sukot, Pesach, and Shavuot) What are we asked to do on these three holidays? (bring offerings to God; see Leviticus 23:33-36 for Sukot offerings)

Holiday Experience Activities (pp. 6-7)

1. Have students begin a running list in their notebook of the different types of Jewish holidays. Instruct them to write each of the following heads on the top of a sheet of paper: *Shalosh Regalim*, Minor Festivals, Fast Days, and *Yamim Noraim*. Then ask them to write a sentence or two about each type of holiday. As they work through the textbook, have students add each new holiday to the appropriate page, along with a brief description of it.

2. Ask a few volunteers to keep a moon diary. Students should go outside every evening and look for the moon. If it is visible, each student should draw a picture of it and the direction he or she had to look to find it. Students should then write down the Jewish and Gregorian dates and the time of each observation. After a few months, have students compare their observations and share them with the rest of the class. Ask students what they can learn from this information. (Students can learn how the moon waxes and wanes each month. They should note that the full moon always falls on the fifteenth of the Jewish month and that the day on which the new moon falls is called Rosh Chodesh, the "Beginning of the Month." Students can also learn that the cycles of the moon do not correspond in any way to the months of the Grego-

rian calendar. Students should be aware that the time of the moonrise changes just as the time of the sunset does. But unlike the sun, the moon might rise in a different direction on different nights.)

3.   Have students research how women celebrate Rosh Chodesh today. Refer students to Resources on page 10. Ask volunteers to create a Rosh Chodesh celebration for the class.

Focus on Focus (p. 8)

1.   Ask students to identify some of the differences between the solar and lunar calendars. (Both have twelve months, but lunar months are shorter–29 or 30 days instead of 30 or 31. The solar year is 365 1/4 days long, whereas the lunar year is only 354 days. The solar leap year adds one day every four years, while the lunar leap year adds a whole month periodically or seven times in a nineteen-year cycle. The cycles of the moon correspond to the lunar months in a consistent way.) Then have students bring in (or provide them with) a combination Jewish-Gregorian calendar. Have them compare and contrast the two calendars by asking them the following questions:

   •   Which information is more prominent, Jewish or secular?

   •   Is the calendar organized mainly according to the Jewish or the Gregorian calendar?

   •   What Jewish information does it provide? What secular information does it give?

   •   Does the calendar give the dates of the Christian holidays?

   •   Is Rosh Chodesh marked in a special way?

   •   How is Shabbat marked? Is Sunday highlighted in any way?

2.   An alternative way to do the previous activity is to conduct a Calendar Treasure Hunt. Ask students to find the dates on which Rosh Chodesh falls this year. Have them then find the names of the Torah portions and the candlelighting times for the weeks on which Rosh Chodesh falls.

3.   Have each student make a decorative calendar showing the seasons, the Jewish holidays, and the Jewish months. You can make this into a year-long project by having students add to their calendar as the class studies each new holiday.

Questions to Think About

1.   Must a person have a Jewish calendar in order to live a Jewish life? Do you use a Jewish calendar to help you live a Jewish life?

2.   Do you think it is appropriate for Jews to celebrate non-Jewish holidays? If your answer is yes, which holidays and under what circumstances?

Which non-Jewish holidays do you celebrate? Can you think of ways in which non-Jewish holidays could be celebrated in Jewish ways?

Closure

Remind students that calendars are important because they help us keep track of both the important events in our lives and the turning of the seasons. Tell students that this textbook will help them learn about each Jewish holiday, how it fits into the cycle of the Jewish year, and how it enriches our lives as Jews.

Enrichment Activities

1. Ask the librarian or rabbi to show students how to use a biblical concordance. (See Resources on page 10.) Look up *new moon* under the entry for "moon" and read the information to the class. Ask students what the entry says about Rosh Chodesh in biblical times.

2. Have students go to the library and do research about other kinds of calendars. Then have them compare and contrast at least three calendars, for example, the Gregorian, Muslim, and Jewish calendars. Students could use a chart like the one below:

Calendar Type	Lunar/Solar Combination	No. of Months	No. of Days in a Month	No. of Days in a Year	Leap Year	Current Year
Gregorian						
Muslim						
Jewish						

3. Bring in a Jewish perpetual calendar. Explain to students that the term *perpetual calendar* is a misnomer because perpetual calendars are not perpetual but cover 100 years or more. Consider showing students a copy of Arthur Spier's *The Comprehensive Calendar, 1900-2000* (Behrman House, 1952) or volume one of the *Encyclopaedia Judaica*, which contains a perpetual calendar that continues until the Gregorian year 2020. Help students find the Hebrew date of their birthday.

More on Calendars

Religious Calendars

Many religions besides Judaism use a calendar other than the Gregorian calendar. They still use ancient calendars because only these calendars record which days are to be set aside for religious observance.

Like the Jewish calendar, the Muslim calendar is lunar, which means it is based on the moon. Muslims count the years from the date their prophet

Mohammed fled from Mecca. The year 1994 corresponded to the year 1415 on the Muslim calendar.

Catholic and Protestant Christians have a calendar based partly on the Gregorian solar calendar (Christmas always falls on December 25) and partly on the Jewish lunar calendar (Easter always occurs around Passover time). Christians follow the Gregorian counting of the years since the birth of Jesus, which is what most Jews think of as the secular date.

The Jewish Calendar

The Jewish calendar has twelve lunar months. Each month begins with the appearance of the new moon, the first sliver of the moon.

The Jewish calendar actually combines the lunar and solar calendars. Twelve lunar months make a year of 354 days. The lunar year is roughly eleven days shorter than the solar year, which has 365 1/4 days. We add an extra month periodically to the Jewish calendar (seven times during a nineteen-year cycle) to keep it even with the solar calendar. The difference between the lunar and solar calendars explains why the holidays fall at different times from year to year and why people talk about the Jewish holidays coming early or late. In fact, the holidays are always on time.

Creating a calendar is a complicated task. In ancient times, Jews did not figure out the calendar in advance. Instead, witnesses who watched for the reappearance of the moon would report their observations to the Sanhedrin (the High Court), which then decided whether a month would be twenty-nine or thirty days long. Later, sometime after 360 C.E., Jewish leaders created a set of rules for the Jewish calendar.

Resources

Cruden, Alexander. *Cruden's Complete Concordance to the Old and New Testaments*, 1930. Reprinted by Zondervan Publishing House, 1949.

Klein, Isaac. *A Guide to Jewish Religious Practice.* New York: The Jewish Theological Seminary, 1979.

Telushkin, Joseph. *Jewish Literacy.* New York: William Morrow and Co., 1991.

On Rosh Chodesh

Danan, Julie Hilton. *The Jewish Parents' Almanac.* Northvale, NJ: Jason Aronson, Inc., 1993, pp. 171-173.

Diamant, Anita. *Living a Jewish Life.* New York: HarperCollins, 1991, pp. 284-285.

Siegel, Richard, Michael Strassfeld, and Sharon Strassfeld. *The First Jewish Catalog.* Philadelphia: The Jewish Publication Society, 1973, pp. 97-99.

Chapter Two

Shabbat

Chapter Summary

- On Shabbat we remember two important biblical events: God rested after creating the world and God freed us from slavery.

- We welcome Shabbat with a blessing over Shabbat candles, a blessing over wine or grape juice (called *Kiddush*), and blessings before and after the meal.

- We are not supposed to work on Shabbat.

- Shabbat concludes with the *Havdalah* ceremony.

Instructional Objectives

Students will be able to:

- Identify and explain the rituals performed at the Shabbat table on Friday evening.

- Demonstrate and explain the parts of the *Havdalah* ceremony.

- List some of the activities that are considered "work" in the *Mishnah*.

- Differentiate between Shabbat *menuchah* and other kinds of rest.

Key Terms

Birkat Hamazon	The blessing after meals.
Challah	The special braided bread that is blessed and eaten on Shabbat.

11

Haftarah	A reading from Prophets that is read or chanted after the Torah reading on Shabbat mornings and festivals.
Hamotzi	The blessing over bread.
Havdalah	Literally, "Separation"; the ceremony conducted on Saturday evening that separates Shabbat from the rest of the week.
Kabbalat Shabbat	Welcoming Shabbat.
Kedushah	Holiness.
Kiddush	The blessing over wine or grape juice.
Lechah Dodi	A song that welcomes the Sabbath bride.
Menuchah	Rest.
Oneg	Joy.
Shamor	Observe.
Zachor	Remember.
Zemirot	Special songs and melodies for Shabbat.

Learning Activities

Materials

Shabbat ritual objects: candles, candlesticks, a challah cover, a *Kiddush* cup, a *Havdalah* candle, a spice box; Bibles; prayer books; art supplies for making ritual objects; a camera; *benschers*.

Opening

Display the Shabbat ritual objects on your desk or elsewhere in the classroom. Briefly explain what each one is. Suggest to students that they conduct a Shabbat Treasure Hunt at home. Ask how many of them think they will be able to find candles, candlesticks, a challah cover, a *Kiddush* cup, a spice box, and/or a *Havdalah* candle. Then ask them if they know how and when each of these ritual objects is used. Explain that in this lesson they will learn about each object, what it is used for, and when it is used.

Story Study (p. 12)

Ask students the following questions:

- Each angel responds to the other angel's prayer by saying "Amen." Why? (The word *amen* comes from the Hebrew *lehamin*, meaning "to believe." The tradition of responding "Amen" to a prayer dates back to the days when not everyone knew the words of the prayers. People who did not know the prayers would listen to a rabbi or another learned person say a prayer and then respond "Amen," meaning "Yes, I believe that, too. That prayer is my prayer, too." Today the custom is to say "Amen" after hearing someone else's blessing [even if one knows the blessing]. Thus each angel, upon hearing the prayer of the other angel, is forced to say "Amen."]

- What do you think is the message of this story? (The message of the story is that our actions carry over from one week to the next, or *mitzvah goreret mitzvah*, "one *mitzvah* leads to another." It is hard to break habits, both good and bad. If we are in the habit of observing Shabbat, it is easy to continue doing so. If we do not observe Shabbat, it is hard to begin. But even a little effort makes it easier to do more. It is possible to change our habits with just a little effort.)

- Do you think the way we celebrate one Shabbat can affect the way we will celebrate the next Shabbat? Explain your answer.

Text Study Review (pp. 13-14)

1.   Ask students the following questions:

- What did God do on the first Shabbat? (On the first Shabbat, God finished the work of creation and rested; God also blessed the seventh day and made it holy.)

- What do you think is the difference between *Zachor*, "Remember," and *Shamor*, "Observe"? (*Shamor*– "Keep," "Observe," or "Guard"–is a more active verb than *Zachor*–"Remember." Remembering is a thought process, whereas observing requires action. *Shamor* has more to do with all the dos and don'ts of Shabbat. *Zachor* is more about the atmosphere, the beauty, the idea of Shabbat.)

2.   Have students find Deuteronomy 5:12-15 in a Bible. Ask them to point out the differences between the way the Fourth Commandment appears in Exodus 20:8-11 and the way it is presented in Deuteronomy 5:12-15. (The first difference is *Zachor*–"Remember"–in Exodus and *Shamor*– "Observe"–in Deuteronomy. In the Deuteronomy passage more emphasis is placed on other animals and slaves resting, which is mentioned twice in verse 14. Also, in the Deuteronomy passage we are reminded that we were once slaves and that God gave us Shabbat as a symbol of our freedom.)

Holiday Experience Activities (pp. 15-18)

1.   First, ask students to make a list of their weekly chores and when they accomplish them. Students should include household duties, homework, taking care of pets, lessons, practice time, etc. Then, suggest that students design a schedule for themselves that would help them accomplish all their chores so that they are free on Friday nights and Saturdays

14

to observe Shabbat. Finally, ask students what they need to do each day in order to be free on Shabbat.

2. Discuss with students which objects on the table and which actions make Shabbat dinner different from dinner on every other night of the week. Suggest that students use a chart like the one below:

Object	Action
A. Candles	A. Light and bless; enjoy and use
B. Wine and *Kiddush* cup	B. Bless and drink
C. Challah	C. Bless and eat

3. According to the *Kiddush* (p. 16), Shabbat is supposed to remind us of two events. Have students look at the text of the *Kiddush* and then ask them to identify those two events. (creation and the Exodus)

4. Ask students the following questions:

    •   What does the word *Havdalah* mean? ("Separation")

    •   How do we use each of our five senses during the *Havdalah* ceremony? (We use our tongue to taste the wine, our nose to smell the spices, our fingers to feel the warmth of the flame, our eyes to see the shadows the candle makes, and our ears to hear the blessings and the sound of the candle being put out in the wine.)

5. Have students study the *Havdalah* ceremony in the textbook (pp. 17-18). They might also want to look at *Gates of Prayer* or another prayer book. Divide students into groups and ask each group to conduct a *Havdalah* ceremony for the class.

6. Ask the art teacher or director of education to help students make one or more Shabbat ritual objects. Encourage students to use different types of materials, for example, watercolor paints, papier-mâché, clay, and construction paper. Set up some Shabbat dinner tables using these objects and take photos to display in the classroom or school or to send home with students.

Focus on Focus (pp. 19-21)

1. Ask students to brainstorm a list of thirty-nine "work" activities that they think are forbidden on Shabbat. They can do this as a class, in pairs, or as individuals. Then have them compare their list with the following list of activities from the *Mishnah*.

39 Categories of Work from *Mishnah Shabbat 7:2*

Ploughing	Dyeing	Cutting to shape
Sowing	Spinning	Writing
Reaping	Weaving operations (3 categories)	Erasing
Sheaf-making		Building
Threshing	Separating into threads	Demolishing
Winnowing	Tying a knot	Kindling a fire
Selecting	Untying a knot	Putting Out a fire
Sifting	Sewing	Putting the finishing touches on a newly manufactured article
Grinding	Tearing	
Kneading	Trapping/Hunting	
Baking	Slaughtering	Carrying from the private to the public domain (or vice versa)
Sheepshearing	Skinning	
Bleaching	Tanning	
Combining raw materials	Scraping pelts	
	Marking Out	

Ask students if any of the activities on their list falls under the categories listed above, for example, doing homework as a type of writing or erasing and washing dishes as a type of bleaching.

2. Ask students if they think the list from the *Mishnah* should be updated. Ask: Why or why not? What new categories would you add?

3. Have students compare the concepts of *menuchah*, *kedushah*, and *oneg*. Ask: How are they the same? How are they different? (*Menuchah*, *kedushah*, and *oneg* are three different aspects of enjoying Shabbat. *Menuchah* is Shabbat rest, a time to relax and enjoy ourselves at the end of a stressful and busy week. As we hurry through our weekday activities, we know that Shabbat will come at the end of the week. *Kedushah* is Shabbat holiness. Shabbat is supposed to be like an island in time, a day set aside for prayer, study, and *menuchah*, "rest." *Oneg* is Shabbat joy. We feel Shabbat joy by spending time with our family, by eating special foods, and by praying, studying, and resting. These three aspects of Shabbat are not the same, but they are related. *Kedushah* and *oneg* are part of the larger concept of *menuchah*.)

4. Instruct students to write in their notebook one or more activities that are examples of *menuchah*, *kedushah*, and *oneg*.

5. Have students evaluate each of the activities listed below. Ask them to categorize each activity according to M for *Menuchah*, O for *Oneg*, K for *Kedushah*, and W for Work. Tell students that some activities may belong in more than one category. Have students compare their answers.

See if the class can come to a consensus about the category to which each activity belongs.

	M	O	K	W
a. Attending Shabbat worship services at the temple.				
b. Gardening in the backyard.				
c. Sharing a meal at home with friends.				
d. Going to the movies with a group of friends.				
e. Watching television.				
f. Going for a walk in the countryside or a park.				
g. Attending a discussion on world peace.				
h. Catching up on the ironing.				
i. Going out to dinner at a restaurant with family.				
j. Lighting Shabbat candles at home.				
k. Pursuing a favorite handicraft (sewing, painting, etc.).				
l. Going to the beach or swim club.				
m. Napping.				
n. Studying the Torah portion of the week.				
o. Reading a book or magazine.				
p. Waxing the car.				
q. Exercising at the health club.				
r. Doing math homework problems.				
s. Strolling and window-shopping in the mall.				
t. Writing checks to pay bills.				

Exploring Times and Places (pp. 21-22)

Here are the words to *Lechah Dodi*, from *Gates of Prayer: The New Union Prayerbook*, page 246.

Lechah dodi likrat kalah,
penei Shabbat nekabelah.
    Beloved, come to meet the bride; beloved, come to greet Shabbat.

Shamor vezachor bedibur echad,
hishmianu El hameyuchad.
Adonai echad ushemo echad,
leshem uletiferet velitehilah.
Lechah dodi...
    Keep and Remember: a single command
    the Only God caused us to hear;

the Eternal is One, God's name is One,
for honor and glory and praise.
Beloved, come to meet the bride; beloved, come to greet Shabbat.

Likrat Shabbat lechu venelechah,
ki hi mekor haberachah.
Merosh mikedem nesuchah,
sof ma'aseh, bemachashavah techilah.
Lechah dodi...
> Come with me to meet Shabbat,
> forever a fountain of blessing.
> Still it flows, as from the start:
> the last of days, for which the first was made.
> Beloved, come to meet the bride; beloved, come to greet Shabbat.

Hitoreri, hitoreri,
ki va orech! kumi, ori,
uri uri, shir daberi,
kevod Adonai alayich niglah.
Lechah dodi...
> Awake, awake,
> your light has come!
> Arise, shine, awake, and sing:
> the Eternal's glory dawns upon you.
> Beloved, come to meet the bride; beloved, come to greet Shabbat.

Bo'i veshalom, ateret ba'alah;
gam besimchah uvetzahalah.
Toch emunei am segulah.
Bo'i chalah! Bo'i chalah!
Lechah dodi...
> Enter in peace, O crown of your husband;
> enter in gladness, enter in joy.
> Come to the people that keeps its faith.
> Enter, O bride! Enter, O bride!
> Beloved, come to meet the bride; beloved, come to greet Shabbat.

Read the English translation to the students and ask them to explain the main idea of each verse in their own words. Ask why they think this song has become such an important part of our Friday night liturgy. (*Lechah Dodi* has become an important part of our liturgy because of its beautiful imagery. The words of the song have also been set to many lovely melodies that people remember all their lives.)

Question to Think About
What does the term *to be holy* mean?

18

Journal Entry

Have students describe their favorite Shabbat memory. If their family does not observe Shabbat (yet), have them describe a memory that they would like to have. Ask students how they would *like* to observe Shabbat.

Closure

Direct students' attention to the quote at the beginning of the chapter on page 11: "More than Israel has kept the Sabbath, the Sabbath has kept Israel." Tell students that this quote comes from the following passage:

> A Jew who feels a real tie with the life of his people throughout the generations will find it utterly impossible to think of the existence of Israel without the Sabbath. One can say without exaggeration that more than Israel has kept the Sabbath, the Sabbath has kept Israel. Had it not been for the Sabbath, which weekly restored to the people their "soul" and weekly renewed their spirit, the weekday afflictions would have pulled them farther and farther downward until they sank to the lowest depths of materialism, as well as ethical and intellectual poverty. Therefore, one need not be a Zionist in order to feel all the traditional sacred grandeur that hovers over this "good gift" and to rise up with might against all who seek to destroy it.

Ask students what they think Ahad Ha-Am meant. Then ask them if they think what Ahad Ha-am wrote is true.

Enrichment Activities

1. Ask students if they have a *benscher* at home. If they do, have them bring the *benscher* to school. For those who do not, bring some *benschers* to school for them to look at. Tell students that a *benscher* is a special booklet that contains *Birkat Hamazon* and Shabbat songs, called *zemirot*. *Benschers* are often given out at weddings and bar/bat mitzvah celebrations. If students found a *benscher* at home, ask them if they (or their parents) remember using the *benscher* at someone's *simchah*. If they do, ask which blessings were said and which songs were sung. Sing or teach some of the songs from the *benscher*.

2. Organize a Shabbat dinner for students and their families. It could be held at the synagogue or in someone's home. The dinner can be catered or potluck (see Activity 3, below). The evening can be as elaborate or as simple as you want. Ask parents to help. The purpose of the dinner is for students to demonstrate their newly acquired knowledge of Shabbat rituals.

3. Food is an integral part of most Jewish holidays, including Shabbat. A typical side dish from Europe is *lokshen* kugel–noodle pudding. Make

arrangements to use the temple's kitchen to cook this dish with students. Consider bringing this dish, along with others, to your class Shabbat dinner. Two versions of this dish appear below.

Lokshen Kugel (Noodle Pudding)

1 lb. medium egg noodles
8 ozs. cream cheese
2 cups sour cream
1 stick margarine, melted
4 eggs
1/2 cup sugar

Topping
2 cups cornflake crumbs
2 tsps. cinnamon
1/4 cup sugar
2 tbsps. melted butter

Preheat the oven to 350°F. Boil the noodles. While they are cooking, use an electric mixer to soften the cream cheese. Add the sour cream, margarine, eggs, and sugar to the cream cheese. Then add the cooked, drained noodles and mix together gently. Grease a 9" x 13" pan. Pour the noodle mixture into the pan. Mix together the topping ingredients and sprinkle on top of the noodle mixture. Bake for 45 minutes.

Parve Lokshen Kugel

Jews who keep kosher do not eat milk products and meat at the same time. If they are having chicken for Shabbat dinner, they serve a *parve* kugel, i.e., a kugel that has no meat or milk ingredients. Below is a recipe for a *parve* noodle kugel.

1/2 lb. wide egg noodles
6 eggs
4 tbsps. *parve* margarine, melted
1/2 cup sugar
1 8-oz. can crushed pineapple
  with juice

1 tsp. vanilla
1 tsp. cinnamon
pineapple rings
maraschino cherries

Preheat the oven to 350°F. Boil the noodles. While they are cooking, combine the eggs and the margarine. Beat well. Add the sugar, crushed pineapple with juice, vanilla, and cinnamon. Mix well. Add the cooked, drained noodles and mix together gently. Grease a 9" x 13" pan. Pour in the noodle mixture. Place pineapple rings on top and put a maraschino cherry in the center of each ring. Bake for 45 minutes.

Resources

Heschel, Abraham Joshua. *The Sabbath.* New York: Farrar, Straus & Giroux, 1951.

Millgram, Abraham E., ed. *Sabbath: The Day of Delight.* Philadelphia: The Jewish Publication Society, 1965.

Perelson, Ruth. *An Invitation to Shabbat.* New York: UAHC Press, 1997.

Stern, Chaim, ed. *Gates of Prayer: The New Union Prayerbook.* New York: CCAR Press, 1975.

Wolfson, Ron. *The Art of Jewish Living: The Shabbat Seder.* New York: Federation of Jewish Mens Clubs, 1985.

Zisenwine, David, and Karen Abramovitz. *The Sabbath: Time and Existence.* Tel Aviv: Everyman's University Publishing House, 1982.

Chapter Three

Rosh Hashanah

Chapter Summary

- Rosh Hashanah, the beginning of the Jewish year, falls on the first of Tishri.
- We celebrate the birthday of the world on Rosh Hashanah, which also marks the beginning of the *Yamim Noraim*, the ten "Days of Awe."
- We welcome Rosh Hashanah with a special meal that includes blessings over the holiday candles, reciting *Kiddush*, and blessings before and after the meal.
- It is a *mitzvah* to hear the sound of the *shofar* on Rosh Hashanah.

Instructional Objectives

Students will be able to:

- Explain the meaning of the High Holy Days as summed up in the *Unetaneh Tokef* prayer.
- Describe the three kinds of notes blown on the *shofar*.
- Identify some of the reasons why we blow the *shofar* on Rosh Hashanah.

Key Terms

Ba'al tekiah	The *shofar* blower.
Selichot	The service of penitence on the Saturday night before Rosh Hashanah.

Shevarim	A set of three blasts of the *shofar*.
Shofar	The ram's horn.
Tashlich	The custom of throwing bread crumbs, symbolizing sins of the past year, into a body of water.
Tefilah	Prayer.
Tekiah	A single blast of the *shofar*.
Tekiah gedolah	A very long *tekiah*.
Teruah	A set of nine very short blasts of the *shofar*.
Teshuvah	Repentance.
Tzedakah	Righteousness; acts of charity.
Unetaneh Tokef	One of the most important Rosh Hashanah prayers, which sums up the meaning of the High Holy Days.
Yamim Noraim	The Days of Awe, which begin on Rosh Hashanah and end with Yom Kippur.
Yom Hadin	The Day of Judgment; another name for Rosh Hashanah.

Learning Activities

Materials

Shofarot; construction paper, markers, and other art supplies for making greeting cards.

Opening

Ask students what types of objects they use to celebrate a birthday. Try to elicit the answer "noisemakers." Ask if they know when the birthday of the world is. Explain that one of the ways we celebrate the birthday of the world is by blowing a horn called a *shofar* on Rosh Hashanah. Ask students if they know what a *shofar* is. Show them one. If possible, let them try blowing it. Tell them in advance that sounding a *shofar* is not easy.

Explain that in this lesson they will learn more about blowing the *shofar*, what the *shofar* blasts mean, and how we celebrate Rosh Hashanah, the birthday of the world.

Story Study (pp. 24-25)

1. Have students act out the story of Reb Yakov's trial. Ask them to consider the following questions:

- What *mitzvot* might Reb Yakov have performed during the past year?
- What would the angels say in his defense?
- What might Reb Yakov's sins have been?
- What would Satan say about them?

2. Ask students to suggest what Reb Yakov might do during the ten Days of Awe in order to be inscribed in the Book of Life.

3. Have students open their notebook and on the left side write across the top of the page Good Deeds and on the right side Bad Deeds. Ask students to imagine themselves standing in the Heavenly Court, just as Reb Yakov did. Have them write down the good deeds they have done during the past year on the credit side of the page and the bad deeds on the debit side. Now ask them what they would do during the ten Days of Awe in order to be inscribed in the Book of Life.

Text Study Review (p. 26)

1. Ask students the following questions:
   - According to the prayer *Unetaneh Tokef*, what happens on Rosh Hashanah and Yom Kippur? (According to *Unetaneh Tokef*, God opens the "book of our days," an imaginary book in which our deeds, both good and bad, are written down. Based on the way we have lived our lives during the past year, God decides our destinies. According to this prayer, God makes decisions about who will live and who will die, who will become rich, and who will be poor, etc. The prayer also tells us that repentance, prayer, and deeds of charity can influence God's decision.)
   - Do human beings have any control over the decisions God makes during the Days of Awe? (According to this prayer, we can influence God's decisions by being repentant, by praying, and by doing *tzedakah*. If we have tried our best to be good and righteous during the year, our names will be written down in the Book of Life.)
   - To what is God compared in this poem? To what are people compared? What does this prayer teach us about God's nature? What does the poet want us to think about? (God is compared to a shepherd, and we are God's flock. God is portrayed as a loving but stern Ruler who expects us to treat one another kindly and justly. This prayer conveys the notion that while God is powerful, deciding the destiny of each creature, we also have some power because we can influence God's decisions. God does not seek "the death of sinners" but desires that we all "turn from their ways and live.")
   - How can we win God's forgiveness? (by repenting, by praying, by doing *tzedakah*, and by turning from our evil ways and following the right path)

24

- Based on this prayer, what are the main themes of the High Holy Days? (first, that our destinies are "written" on Rosh Hashanah and "sealed" on Yom Kippur; second, that we have some power to change our destinies by repenting, praying, and doing righteous acts; third, that God does not want to punish us for our sins but wants us to turn from our sinful paths and live righteous lives)

2. Parts of this prayer are frightening and parts of it make the reader feel secure and safe. Have students work as a group to identify the parts that are frightening, those that are soothing, and those that are neither. The text of *Unetaneh Tokef* that appears in the book is reproduced below. Use the table to record students' reactions. F stands for "Frightening," S stands for "Safe" or "Secure," and N stands for "Neither."

	F	S	N

Let us proclaim the sacred power of this day;
It is awesome and full of dread.
For on this day Your reign is exalted,
Your throne is established in everlasting love....
You open the book of our days, and what is written there speaks for itself, for it is signed by every person....
As the shepherd seeks out his flock, and makes the sheep pass under his staff, so do You count and consider every soul, setting the boundary of every creature's life, and deciding its destiny.
On Rosh Hashanah it is written, on Yom Kippur it is sealed:
How many shall pass on, how many shall come to be;
Who shall live and who shall die....
But repentance, prayer, and *tzedakah* save us from the severe decree.
This is Your glory: You are slow to anger, ready to forgive. *Adonai*, it is not the death of sinners You seek, but that they should turn from their ways and live....
Humanity's origin is dust, and dust is our end.
Each of us is a shattered pot, grass that must wither, a flower that will fade, a shadow moving on, a cloud passing by, a particle of dust floating on the wind, a dream soon forgotten.
But You are the Ruler, the everlasting God!

Holiday Experience Activities (pp. 27-29)

1. Ask students why we choose to begin the new year with something sweet. Tell students that another traditional Rosh Hashanah food is a round challah, which sometimes contains raisins, instead of the usual braided loaf. Ask students what they think is the significance of a round raisin challah. (The round challah signifies the cycle of the year. The raisins sweeten it, symbolizing the desire for a sweet new year.)

2. If possible, gather several *shofarot* for students to see and touch. Here are some questions for you to ask and some activities for students to do:

   - What is a *shofar?* (A *shofar* is a special horn made from a ram's horn.)

   - Have students compare and contrast the *shofarot*. Ask them what all the *shofarot* have in common. (All *shofarot* have been hollowed out and prepared in such a way that they can be blown like a trumpet, but they do not have a mouthpiece. *Shofarot* come in different shades, ranging from off-white to tan, brown, and black. They come in different sizes, too, from not much longer than your forearm to very long and twisted. The completed surface of a *shofar* can be rough or smooth, although smooth is more common.)

   - Ask students to do some research in the library in order to learn about how a *shofar* is made. (For example, have them look at pages 71 and 72 of Richard Siegel and Michael and Sharon Strassfeld's *The First Jewish Catalog.*)

   - According to Maimonides, why do we blow the *shofar?* (Maimonides says that the *shofar* wakes us up and reminds us to work at being better people. We should give up bad habits and try to do important, worthwhile things. See also Resources on page 27.)

   - Rabbi Saadia Gaon gave ten reasons for blowing the *shofar*. The text lists four of them. Ask students if they can think of two or three more reasons. (to announce the beginning of the ten Days of Repentance; to encourage us to turn to God in *teshuvah*; to remind us of the destruction of the Temple)

Family Album Focus (p. 29)

Rabbi Wylen describes the creative way in which his family observes the custom of *Tashlich*. Divide the class into groups of two or three. Ask each group to design its own creative *Tashlich* ceremony. Have the class vote on which one of the creative ceremonies they will do together. (For example, students might write their misdeeds on paper and then make sailboats out of the paper; or students might look for prayers, poems, stories, and songs that speak of forgiveness and weave them into a service; or students might take a walk to a nearby river, stream, or other body of water and cast bread crumbs into the water; or students might recite a list of their misdeeds and pretend to throw them into the water.)

Focus on Focus (p. 30)

Have each student design and create a Rosh Hashanah greeting card, using an appropriate greeting as the text. Provide students with an array of art supplies for making the cards, e.g., crayons or markers, construction paper, glitter and glue, glossy magazines with pictures and advertisements. When students are finished, have them send their card to a friend, take it home to their parents, or put it up on the classroom wall.

Something to Think About

Have students listen to a *shofar* being blown. Ask them what the *shofar* says to them. Then have them imagine that they are the *shofar*. Suggest that they write their answer in the form of a letter from the *shofar* to them.

Closure

The Summary on page 30 points out that Rosh Hashanah is also called *Yom Hadin*, the "Day of Judgment." Explain that judgment is one of the main themes of this holiday. Judgment, repentance, and forgiveness are also the themes of Yom Kippur, the holy day that will be studied in the next chapter.

Enrichment Activities

1.   The *shofar* is blown during a special section of the Rosh Hashanah service called the Shofar Service. Have students look at the Shofar Service in a High Holy Day prayer book, e.g., *Gates of Repentance*, New York: CCAR Press, 1978, pp. 138-151. Ask students to identify the three parts of the Shofar Service. (*Malchuyot, Zichronot, Shofarot*) Then have them fill in the chart below:

Name	Main Purpose/Theme
Malchuyot (Sovereignty)	
Zichronot (Remembrance)	
Shofarot (Revelation)	

2.   Have students design a bulletin board or another display (e.g., a poster or comic strip) about the *shofar*. Possible ideas include: the reasons for

blowing the *shofar*; modern things to which a *shofar* might be compared (e.g., an alarm clock, a judge); things the *shofar* might inspire us to do or to change.

3. Invite a *ba'al tekiah* to school to blow the *shofar* for the class. Ask the *ba'al tekiah* to tell the class how he or she learned to blow the *shofar*. Ask if there are any students who are interested in learning how to blow the *shofar*. If there are, ask the *ba'al tekiah* to give these students a lesson in *shofar* blowing.

4. It is traditional to eat other sweet foods besides apples and honey on Rosh Hashanah. One delicious treat that many people serve is honey cake. Here is an easy recipe for honey cake.

Honey Cake

1 1/2 cups honey	1 tsp. baking soda
1 cup coffee	2 1/2 tsps. baking powder
4 eggs	1/2 tsp. allspice
4 tbsps. vegetable oil	1 tsp. cinnamon
1 cup brown sugar	1/4 tsp. nutmeg
3 1/2 cups flour	1/4 tsp. ground cloves
1/2 cup raisins	1/2 cup chopped walnuts
1/8 tsp. salt	

Preheat the oven to 300° F. Grease a 9″ x 13″ pan. Bring the honey and coffee to a near-boil in a saucepan. In a bowl beat the eggs. Stir the oil into the eggs and add the brown sugar a little at a time. In another bowl mix together all the dry ingredients. Into this bowl stir in about 1/3 of the egg mixture, then 1/3 of the honey mixture. Repeat this procedure two more times. Mix well. Pour the batter into the prepared baking pan. Bake for about one hour. Allow the cake to cool completely before serving it.

Resources

Agnon. S.Y. *Days of Awe.* New York: Schocken Books, 1965, pp. 64-74.

Chavel, Charles, translator. *Thoughts for Rosh Hashanah from the Writings of Ramban and Rabbeinu Bachya.* New York: Shilo Publishing House, Inc., 1987, pp. 30-36.

Elkins, Dov Peretz, ed. *Moments of Transcendence: Inspirational Readings for Rosh Hashanah.* Northvale, NJ: Jason Aronson, Inc., 1992, pp. 209-248.

Siegel, Richard, Michael Strassfeld, and Sharon Strassfeld. *The First Jewish Catalog.* Philadelphia: The Jewish Publication Society, 1973, pp. 71-72.

Stern, Chaim, ed. *Gates of Repentance.* New York: CCAR Press, 1978.

Chapter Four

Yom Kippur

Chapter Summary

- Yom Kippur is the Day of Atonement. It is the holiest day in the Jewish calendar, as well as a day of fasting, rest, and prayer.

- Yom Kippur occurs on the tenth of Tishri. It is the last day of the ten Days of Awe.

- On Yom Kippur we atone for our sins and promise to improve our behavior.

Instructional Objectives

Students will be able to:

- Understand the meaning of the word *covenant*.

- Explain the covenant as it is described in the Yom Kippur Torah portion.

- List the three steps to *teshuvah*.

Key Terms

Chet	A sin.
Kohen Gadol	The High Priest.
Kol Nidre	Literally, "All Vows"; the famous Yom Kippur eve prayer that asks God to release us from any of our unkept promises.
Teshuvah	Literally, "turning" or "returning"; commonly translated as "repentance."

Vidui   A confession.

Yizkor   A memorial service recited on Yom Kippur
                             and Shavuot, as well as on the last day
                             of Sukot and Pesach.

Learning Activities

Materials

A tape of *Kol Nidre* and a tape deck (see Opening below); butcher paper and
markers; prayer books.

Opening

Play a tape recording of *Kol Nidre* without telling students anything about it
in advance. A fine recording of *Kol Nidre* can be found in *Yamin Noraim Highlights*, an audiocassette and compact disc that is available from Transcontinental Music Publications, UAHC, 838 Fifth Avenue, New York, NY 10021. Ask
students if they recognize the prayer. Then have students listen to the melody
again with their eyes closed. Ask them how it makes them feel and what it
makes them think about.

Explain that *Kol Nidre* is the prayer that "introduces" the themes of
Yom Kippur on the eve of that holy day. The class will study these themes
more thoroughly as they discuss this chapter on Yom Kippur.

Story Study (pp. 32-33)

Ask students the following questions:

- Why didn't Jonah want to go to Ninevah? (Jonah didn't want to go
  to Ninevah because he did not care about its people and didn't see
  why he was the one who had to go and tell them to repent.)

- Why do you think God sent a huge fish to swallow Jonah? Do you
  think that Jonah learned anything from spending three days in the
  belly of the huge fish? If he did, what was it he learned? (God sent
  the big fish to swallow Jonah in order to scare him and save him at
  the same time. God wanted to make Jonah think about all that he
  had and had not done and how his actions had affected the others
  on the ship. When he was inside the fish, Jonah had time to think:
  He had time to wonder if he would ever get out of the fish. He had
  time to reconsider whether he should have done what God had asked.
  Jonah learned that you cannot run away from God.)

- What lesson did God teach Jonah through the gourd plant? (Jonah
  learned that God cares about all living things regardless of whether
  or not they are aware of God's Presence.)

- What lessons can the story of Jonah teach us? (We can learn the
  same lessons that Jonah learned: We cannot run away from God or

from doing the right thing. God is compassionate and wants us, like the people of Ninevah, to mend our ways. God gives us second chances. God cares about all living things.)

Text Study Review (pp. 34-35)

1. Ask students to describe the covenant that the Israelites made with God.

2. Explain that in this Torah portion, Moses is telling the Israelites what God said. We are told that the Israelites accepted the covenant, but the text does not tell us what they thought or said. Have pairs of students role-play two Israelites discussing the new covenant. This activity could be done first as a writing assignment in order to give students a chance to develop their ideas.

3. The text tells us that we, too, are partners in the covenant. Usually people are given the chance to ask questions before they agree to something. Find out from students what questions they would have liked to ask Moses or God before they accepted the covenant.

4. Explain to students that a covenant is a very special set of promises that two parties, individuals or groups, make to each other. In this text study section, God makes a covenant with the people of Israel that is contingent upon their keeping God's commandments. Consider reading other passages from Deuteronomy 29 and 30 to the class and asking students to draw up a chart with two columns labeled We Promise and God Promises. Have students list the promises each party makes to the other in Deuteronomy.

Holiday Experience Activities (pp. 36-38)

1. Ask students the following questions:

    *   What are the three steps to *teshuvah*? (confession, which means admitting that we have done wrong; regret, which means being truly sorry for what we have done; making a vow, which means we intend never to repeat the misdeed)

    *   Why are all three steps necessary? (According to Judaism, all three steps are required because *teshuvah* is a process. It does not entail just saying you are sorry because we all say "I'm sorry" several times a day for many little things. The process of *teshuvah* demands that we think about the "big" things we have done wrong and then change the way we live our lives.)

    *   Judaism teaches that it is never too late for a person to do *teshuvah*. Do you agree? Why or why not?

2. Have students look at the passage from Isaiah on page 38. Ask them to list the kinds of ethical behavior that Isaiah believes should be part of the fast. (Isaiah expects us to free slaves, feed the hungry, provide shel-

ter to the homeless, give clothes to those who do not have any, and never hide from our fellow human beings.)

3. Have students read *First Fast* by Barbara Cohen in order to gain some insight into the meaning of the Yom Kippur fast. Ask students to discuss what the fast meant to the two boys in the story. *First Fast* is available from the UAHC Press, 838 Fifth Avenue, New York, NY 10021, 888-489-8242.

Focus on Focus (p. 40)

Read to students the text of *Kol Nidre* that appears below and then ask them if they think the story of the Marranos who gathered to chant the *Kol Nidre* secretly makes the prayer more meaningful to us today. Have them explain their answer.

KOL NIDRE

Let our vows and oaths, all the promises we make and the
obligations we incur to You, O God, between this Yom Kippur
and the next, be null and void should we, after honest effort,
find ourselves unable to fulfill them. Then may we be absolved
of them.

Exploring Times and Places (pp. 41-42)

1. Ask students what a scapegoat is and from where this idea originated.

2. Tell students that we no longer send a goat into the desert to symbolically carry our sins away. Ask them to suggest a symbolic ceremony they can perform that's more appropriate for our time.

Questions to Think About

Have students turn back to the Text Study section on pages 34 and 35. Ask: Why do you think we read this Torah portion on Yom Kippur? What is the power given to every human being? What does this power have to do with Yom Kippur?

Journal Entry

Have students complete the following statements, based on the three steps to *teshuvah*:

I admit that I...

I am sorry that I...

I promise that I will never again...

Closure

Do the exercise on page 39 of the text with students. Then discuss what the activity teaches us about Yom Kippur.

Enrichment Activities

1. Have students look at the *vidui* in a High Holy Day prayer book, particularly the *Al Chet* section, which has been reproduced below from *Gates of Repentance*, pages 271-272. Then ask students to compose their own *Al Chet*, using the sins listed in the actual prayer as well as ones pertaining to their own life, school, and community.

AL CHET

The sin we have committed against You under duress or by choice,

The sin we have committed against You consciously or unconsciously,

And the sin we have committed against You openly or secretly.

The sin we have committed against You in our thoughts,

The sin we have committed against You with our words,

And the sin we have committed against You by the abuse of power.

For all these, O God of mercy, forgive us, pardon us, grant us atonement!

The sin we have committed against You by hardening our hearts,

The sin we have committed against You by profaning Your name,

And the sin we have committed against You by disrespect for parents and teachers.

The sin we have committed against You by speaking slander,

The sin we have committed against You by dishonesty in our work,

And the sin we have committed against You by hurting others in any way.

For all these, O God of mercy, forgive us, pardon us, grant us atonement!

2. Isaiah emphasizes ethical behavior. Ask students to think about the difference between ritual *mitzvot* and ethical *mitzvot* by doing the following exercise. Show students the following list of Jewish activities. Have them identify them as Ritual *Mitzvot*, Ethical *Mitzvot*, or Both.

	R	E	B
Lighting Shabbat candles			
Giving *tzedakah*			
Saying prayers in synagogue			
Learning Torah			
Wearing a *kipah*			
Comforting a sad friend			
Building a *sukah*			
Helping at a shelter for the homeless			
Making friends at school with an unpopular child			
Saying *Hamotzi* before eating			
Doing a chore for one's parents without being asked			
Resting on Shabbat			
Not eating pork			
Helping run a Purim carnival			

Resources

Cohen, Barbara. *First Fast.* New York: UAHC Press, 1987.

Greenberg, Sidney, and Jonathan D. Levine, eds. *The New Mahzor.* Bridgeport, CT: Media Judaica, 1978.

Levy, Richard N., ed. *On Wings of Awe.* Washington, D.C.: B'nai Brith Hillel Foundations, 1985.

Stern, Chaim, ed. *Gates of Repentance.* New York: CCAR Press, 1978.

Chapter Five

Sukot

Chapter Summary

- Sukot is celebrated for seven days, beginning on the fifteenth of Tishri, five days after Yom Kippur.

- Sukot, also called the Feast of Booths, is one of the *Shalosh Regalim*, the "Three Pilgimage Festivals."

- Sukot has two other names: *Chag Ha'asif*, the "Festival of the Harvest," and *Zeman Simchatenu*, the "Time of Our Joy."

- During Sukot we remember how God protected the Israelites while they wandered in the Sinai Desert.

- It is traditional to build a *sukah*, a temporary booth, to use during this holiday.

- We rejoice on Sukot with a *lulav* and *etrog*.

Instructional Objectives

Students will be able to:

- Identify all the names for Sukot and explain their meaning.

- Describe the characteristics of a *sukah*.

- List the four species and explain how to wave a *lulav*.

- Give some of the reasons for building a *sukah*.

36

Key Terms

Arba'ah minim	The four species; consists of the *lulav*, *etrog*, willow twigs, and myrtle twigs.
Beruchim Habaim	A greeting that means "Welcome."
Bet Hamikdash	The Holy Temple.
Chag Ha'asif	The Festival of the Harvest.
Chol Hamoed	The middle days of Sukot; half-holidays. Pesach also has *Chol Hamoed*.
Etrog	A citron fruit; one of the four species.
Hachag	The Festival, one of the names for Sukot.
Kohelet	The Book of Ecclesiastes, which is read on Sukot.
Lulav	A palm branch from a young date palm.
Sukah	A temporary outdoor booth built in observance of Sukot.
Sechach	The greens for the roof of the *sukah*.
Simchah	Literally, "joy"; a happy event.
Ushpizin	Literally, an "Invitation"; refers to the symbolic "guests" we invite to our *sukah*, consisting of fourteen of our great Jewish ancestors.
Zeman Simchatenu	The Time of Our Joy.

Learning Activities

Materials

Butcher paper, oaktag, markers; Popsicle sticks, glue, a shoe box, and additional art supplies for making a *sukah* and *sukah* decorations.

Opening

Ask students if they have ever planted vegetables in their garden during the summer. Ask: How did you feel after you had harvested your vegetables? How do you think a farmer feels after he or she has brought in a bountiful harvest?

Ask students if they have ever gone camping or slept outside in their backyard. Ask: What was it like to sleep under the stars? How did you feel when you lay on your back looking up at the sky?

Tell students that both harvesting fruits and vegetables and looking up at the stars are part of the festival of Sukot, but don't explain why. Students will return to the above questions in the closing activity.

Story Study (pp. 44-45)

1. Ask students the following questions:

   - What is a miracle? (A miracle is an unexplainable, fantastic occurrence–a supernatural event. According to the *American Heritage Dictionary* [Houghton Mifflin, 1983], a miracle is 1. An extraordinary or unusual event that is considered to be a manifestation of divine or supernatural power. 2. An event that excites admiration, awe, or wonder.)

   - Why did God perform miracles for the Israelites? (God performed miracles to give the people a reason to believe in the Divine. God provided miracles to help them survive. Perhaps these events weren't really miracles–that is, unexplainable events–but because the Children of Israel couldn't explain them, they called them miracles.)

   - What were the miracles that God provided for the Israelites while they wandered in the desert? (The three miracles that God provided in the desert are a cloud that protected the Israelites from the sun; manna for the Israelites to eat; and a well that gave them water to drink.)

   - Did the Israelites consider these to be miracles or did they expect God to provide for them since God took them out of Egypt? (This discussion could focus on the definition of the word *miracle*. Ask students if they think these "gifts" were miracles. Ask: Are these examples of unexplainable events that the Israelites *called* miracles? Can these miracles be explained today?)

   - Do you believe in miracles? Do miracles happen today? If your answer is yes, do you think these miracles are like the miracles of biblical times? If your answer is no, why not?

2. The story says that God provided the miracles to all the Israelites because of the goodness and faith of Moses, Aaron, and Miriam. Ask students to think of several people whom they admire. Have them list the ways in which the world is a better and happier place because of these individuals.

3. Ask students what they think this story has to do with Sukot. (Because the *sukah* is a symbol of protection in Jewish tradition, it, too, reminds us of how God protected the Israelites in the wilderness during their travels.)

Text Study Review (p. 46)

Zechariah says that one day all the nations of the world will celebrate Sukot. Ask students the following questions about Zechariah's statement:

- Which Jewish holiday have other nations (non-Jews) already accepted? (Shabbat, the concept of a day of rest once a week)

- What are some of the Jewish teachings and practices that you think all people should accept?

- How is the world like a *sukah*? (Both are fragile. Just as a strong wind or rain can demolish a fragile *sukah*, so a global war can destroy our fragile world. A *sukah* can also symbolize peace, which is fragile and easily destroyed.)

- Why do you think Zechariah chose Sukot as the festival that all the nations of the world will celebrate? (Sukot is a holiday that celebrates peace, something that the peoples of all nations desire.)

- Why do you think we read this text on Sukot? (We read it because Zechariah's expression of his desire for peace includes the *sukah* as a symbol of peace.)

Holiday Experience Activities (pp. 47-49)

1. Have students list the steps for making a *sukah* on a piece of butcher paper. Then divide the class into small groups and have each group draw a poster of its "ideal" *sukah* on oaktag. Provide students with an assortment of colored markers. Encourage them to embellish their *sukot* without violating the rules for making a *sukah*. When they're done, have each group "present" its *sukah* to the rest of the class.

2. Have students build three-dimensional *sukot* out of various materials (e.g., Popsicle sticks, twigs collected from outside, etc.). Another idea is to have students use a shoe box and concentrate on decorating a miniature *sukah*.

3. Go to the library with students to research plant species that are native to Israel. Have students make illustrated posters of the four species we wave on Sukot.

Family Album Focus (p. 50)

It is traditional to invite guests to our *sukah*. Ask: If you could invite any Jewish person from any time in history to have dinner with you in the *sukah*, whom would you choose? Why? Which questions would you want to ask this person?

Focus on Focus (p. 51)

The Torah commands us to rejoice on Sukot. Ask: How can the Torah command a feeling? How do we rejoice on Sukot? What if we don't feel like being happy? What are some of the things we can do to make ourselves happy?

Exploring Times and Places (p. 52)

1. Tell students that Jerusalem has been central to Jewish thought and worship since biblical times. Whole books have been written about its importance to the Jewish people. Ask students why they think Jerusalem has been and continues to be so important to the Jews.

2. Have students do research in the library to find out how the ancient Israelites worshiped God in the Holy Temple. Refer students to Resources below. Ask: How do we worship God today?

Journal Entry

If any students have visited Jerusalem, have them write down their impressions of that city. Ask those who have never been to Jerusalem to interview someone who has been there. Have students write down that person's impressions of Jerusalem.

Closure

Return to the questions you asked students in the Opening of this lesson. Now that students have learned about Sukot, ask them what these questions have to do with Sukot.

Tell students that one custom many children like to observe is the custom of sleeping in the *sukah* if it is warm enough. Consider planning a special party in your temple's *sukah* or in someone's backyard *sukah*. If it is a warm autumn, consider sleeping in the *sukah* or at least staying out in the *sukah* very late so that students can see the stars through its roof.

Enrichment Activities

1. The *haftarah* portion that is read on the Shabbat during Sukot is taken from the Book of Ezekiel. It is a difficult passage, but you may want to explore it with students to see what Ezekiel has to say. See Ezekiel 38:18-39:16. Have students do research about the concepts of Armageddon and the Messiah/Messianic Age. Refer students to the Resources below.

2. Although Sukot does not have any specific dishes or foods associated with it, in Israel, Jews make it a point of eating from the seven species mentioned in the Torah. The seven species are pomegranates, olives, dates, grapes, wheat, barley, and honey. See Deuteronomy 8:7-8. Plan with your class a Seven Species Feast for this holiday. Invite parents to share the feast in the synagogue's *sukah*.

Resources

On Building a Sukah

Siegel, Richard, Michael Strassfeld, and Sharon Strassfeld. *The First Jewish Catalog*. Philadelphia: The Jewish Publication Society, 1973.

Strassfeld, Michael. *The Jewish Holidays*. New York: Harper & Row, 1985.

40

On Armageddon and the Messiah

Borowitz, Eugene. *Liberal Judaism*. New York: UAHC Press, 1984.

Telushkin, Joseph. *Jewish Literacy*. New York: William Morrow and Co., Inc., 1991.

On Jerusalem

Ben-Arieh, Yehoshua. *Jerusalem in the 19th Century: The Old City*. New York: St. Martin's Press, 1984.

_____. *Jerusalem in the 19th Century: Emergence of the New City*. New York: St. Martin's Press, 1986.

Millgram, Abraham. *Jerusalem Curiosities*. Philadelphia: The Jewish Publication Society, 1990.

Schiller, Ely, ed. *The First Photographs of Jerusalem: The Old City*. Jerusalem: Ariel Publishing House, 1978.

_____. *The First Photographs of Jerusalem: The New City*. Jerusalem: Ariel Publishing House, 1979.

Uris, Leon, and Jill Uris. *Jerusalem: Song of Songs*. Garden City, NY: Doubleday, 1981.

Vilnay, Zev. *Legends of Jerusalem*. Philadelphia: The Jewish Publication Society, 1973.

Chapter Six

Simchat Torah

Chapter Summary

- Simchat Torah is celebrated on the day after Sukot ends. For some Jews, this means the eighth day after Sukot begins; for others, it means the ninth day after Sukot begins.

- On Sukot we read the very last verses of the Torah and then begin the cycle of Torah readings over again with the first verses of Genesis.

- The Torah is written by hand on parchment by a *sofer*, a scribe.

- During services on Simchat Torah, we parade around the synagogue seven times with the Torah(s).

Instructional Objectives

Students will be able to:

- Identify the two passages of the Torah that we read on Simchat Torah.

- Explain why we read those two passages–that is, why we celebrate Simchat Torah.

- Describe the Torah and compare the Torah to a traditional book.

- Explain the difference between the Torah service on Simchat Torah and the Torah service on Shabbat.

Key Terms

Hakafah (pl. Hakafot)   The carrying of the Torah scrolls in a procession around the synagogue.

Hallel (Psalms 113 to 118)	Special psalms of praise, recited or sung on festivals.
Parashat hashavua	The weekly (Torah) portion.
Sefer	A book.
Sefer Torah (pl. Sifre Torah)	The Torah scroll.
Shemini Atzeret	The Eighth Day of Assembly.
Sofer	A scribe; one who is trained in the art of Hebrew calligraphy.
Talmud Torah	The Study of Torah.

Learning Activities

Materials

Butcher paper and markers; a *Sefer Torah*.

Opening

Help students compile a list of everything they know about the Torah. Write their answers on a piece of butcher paper or poster board. Tell students that they will evaluate the list, correct it, and add to it after they have studied about Simchat Torah.

Story Study (p. 54)

1.   Ask students the following questions:

   • Why do you think Akiva decided to study Torah at the age of forty? (Many parents become motivated to learn Hebrew when their children start Hebrew school. In Akiva's day, not everyone went to school, as is customary today. Maybe Akiva decided that learning to read and write was something he really wanted to do.)

   • What kinds of things motivate people to learn at a younger age? At a more advanced age? (A child's motivation to learn is innate, at least until he or she starts school. Children are like sponges: Everything is a learning experience for them. As they get older, their motivation to learn is shaped more by external forces: They strive for good grades to please their teachers and parents, to keep up with their friends, and to make honor roll. For some, the satisfaction of getting a good grade is in itself a motivating factor. As we become older, the motivation for learning becomes more specific: We study to earn a degree, to get a promotion, to fill in a gap in our knowledge, to keep up with our children, and to motivate our children.

2.   Tell students that Akiva became an important teacher. Suggest that they think about the special teachers they have known. Ask them what made these teachers special.

3. Many stories are told about what a wise teacher Akiva became. Have students go to the library and find another story about Akiva. Refer students to Resources on page 45 for some suggestions. Read two or more of the stories to the students. Ask students if the stories have anything in common. Also ask what the story in the textbook and the other stories reveal about Akiva's personality.

4. Have students ask their parents and grandparents how they learned Torah. Then have students compare the way their elders learned Torah with the way they themselves are learning Torah.

Text Study Review (pp. 55-56)

1. Ask students the following questions:

   • Which passages of the Torah do we read on Simchat Torah? Why? (On Simchat Torah we read the final verses of Deuteronomy and the opening verses of Genesis as we conclude the annual cycle of Torah readings and begin the cycle over again.)

   • How did Moses pass on his position as leader of the Israelites? (Moses passed on his authority by laying his hands upon Joshua.)

   • How has the Torah been passed down from one generation to the next? (The Torah has been passed down by parents who teach its values and lessons to their children, who in turn teach it to their children, and so on. Parents have also hired instructors to teach the values, history, and lessons of Judaism to their children.)

2. Ask students to interview their parents and grandparents once again and pose the following questions:

   • How has each generation of our family passed the Torah on to the next generation?

   • Has the understanding of Torah changed from one generation to the next?

   • In what ways has it changed?

   • Why has it changed?

Holiday Experience Activities (pp. 57-59)

1. Ask students:

   • What are some of the differences between a modern book and a *Sefer Torah*? (A *Sefer Torah* was and still is written by hand, whereas a book is printed on a printing press. A *Sefer Torah* is written on parchment, whereas a book is printed on paper. A *Sefer Torah* is in the form of a scroll, whereas a book is bound together with glue and/or thread and has pages to turn. A *Sefer Torah* is usually more fragile than a book.)

- Why do we continue to read from a *Sefer Torah* even though it is easier to read the text from a book? (We continue to read from a *Sefer Torah* because our Jewish ancestors read from it.)

2. Ask the rabbi to show a *Sefer Torah* to students. Let them see the Hebrew text, and have the rabbi explain how a *Sefer Torah* is put together. Point out the columns of text and the paragraphs. If possible, show the students a "special" passage like the Song of the Sea or the Ten Commandments.

3. Ask students to attend their synagogue on Simchat Torah. Afterward, have them describe how their synagogue celebrated the holiday. Ask:

   - Who read from the Torah?

   - Did congregants dance with the Torah?

   - Was there a processional (*hakafah*)? How many *hakafot* were there?

Focus on Focus (pp. 60-61)

Ask students why some Jews observe Simchat Torah on the eighth day after Sukot and others celebrate it on the ninth. (In ancient times, rabbis did not know exactly when the holidays began because the calendar was not written down. The Torah tells us to observe Sukot for seven days. After Sukot comes Shemini Atzeret, to which the rabbis added a second day. In about the tenth century, the second day of Shemini Atzeret became a separate holiday, Simchat Torah. Today, traditional Jews observe Sukot for seven days, Shemini Atzeret for one day, and Simchat Torah for one day. Liberal Jews observe Sukot for seven days and celebrate Shemini Atzeret and Simchat Torah on the same day, the eighth day after Sukot begins.)

Exploring Times and Places (p. 62)

Ask students what message we communicate to the children who participate in the consecration ceremony. (By honoring young children during this ceremony, we are showing them how important Jewish education is to us. We are saying that we hope they grasp the importance the Jewish community places on their Jewish education.)

Questions to Think About

1. Ask students who have participated in a consecration ceremony: Do you remember your consecration? Would you describe it to the class?

2. What have you learned about the Torah from your parents and grandparents?

3. What would you like to teach your own children about Jewish tradition? What would you like to teach them about the Torah?

Closure

Return to the list that students compiled in the Opening of this lesson. Ask them if their ideas about the Torah were accurate. Ask: What can you add to the list? What needs to be changed?

Conclude by explaining that the Torah is the center of Judaism. The traditions of Judaism, symbolized by the Torah, have been passed down from one generation to the next for thousands of years. Students should feel proud that they are another link in that chain of tradition.

Enrichment Activities

1. If possible, arrange for the class to visit a *sofer*, or invite a *sofer* to come to the school. Have students watch the *sofer* work. Encourage them to ask questions about how a Torah is made. Have the *sofer* show them the tools that are used for making a Torah.

2. Ask the art teacher to conduct a bookmaking workshop with students.

Resources

On Being a Sofer

Ray, Eric. *Sofer, The Story of a Torah Scroll.* Los Angeles: Torah Aura Productions, 1995.

On Rabbi Akiva

Bin Gorion, Micha Joseph. *Mimekor Yisrael: Selected Classical Jewish Folktales.* Bloomington, IN: Indiana University Press, 1990, pp. 80-81.

Goldin, Barbara Diamond. *A Child's Book of Midrash.* Northvale, NJ: Jason Aronson, Inc., 1990, pp. 61-68.

Klagsbrun, Francine. *Voices of Wisdom.* New York: Pantheon Books, 1980.

Patai, Raphael. *Gates to the Old City: A Book of Jewish Legends.* Detroit: Wayne State University Press, 1981, pp. 538-539.

Chapter Seven

Chanukah

Chapter Summary

- Chanukah, the Festival of Lights, is celebrated for eight days, beginning on the twenty-fifth of Kislev.
- On Chanukah we remember the victory of Judah Maccabee and the miracle of the one small vial of oil.
- Chanukah celebrates our right to practice our religion free of persecution.
- On each night during the eight days of Chanukah, we light candles in a special menorah called a *chanukiah*.

Instructional Objectives

Students will be able to:

- Relate at least three facts about the origins of Chanukah.
- Translate/define the word *Chanukah*.
- Explain the difference between a menorah and a *chanukiah*.
- Demonstrate the correct way to light a *chanukiah*.
- Identify the letters on a *dreidel* and explain how to play the Dreidel Game.

Key Terms

Chanukiah (pl. Chanukiot)	An eight-branched Chanukah lamp, with a place for a ninth candle that lights the others.

Dreidel	A four-sided top, used in a Chanukah game.
Latkes	Potato pancakes.
Menorah	A seven- or eight-branched candelabra.
Nes Gadol Hayah Sham	Literally, "A Great Miracle Happened There."
Shamash	The "helper" candle that is used to light all the others.
Sufganiot	Jelly doughnuts.

Learning Activities

Materials

Books on Jewish ceremonial art; construction paper, aluminum foil, Popsicle sticks, pipe cleaners, and other lightweight materials.

Opening

Discuss the words *freedom* and *assimilation* with students. Ask them some of the following questions about the two terms: What do the words mean? What do they mean to us as Jews? What do they mean to us as Americans? What do they have to do with Chanukah? Have students write down their answer to the last question. After students have finished studying this chapter, have them compare the answers they gave with what they have learned.

Story Study (pp. 64-66)

Ask students the following questions:

- What did the Jews do when the Greeks tried to force them to violate Shabbat and bow down to idols? (Some Jews did what the Greeks told them and assimilated into Greek society. Others, led by Judah Maccabee, resisted and fought for the right to maintain and follow their customs.)

- What would you do if someone tried to force you to bow down to an idol or do something else that violated your beliefs?

- What does Sukot have to do with the origin of Chanukah? (When Judah Maccabee and his followers were hiding in the Judean hills, they could not offer sacrifices in the Temple on the eight days of Sukot.)

- What is the miracle of Chanukah? (The traditional miracle of Chanukah is that the small vial of oil with the seal of the High Priest, which was enough to relight the menorah for only one day, lasted for eight days. The fact that a small band of Jewish rebels had defeated the mighty Greek army was also a miracle.)

Text Study Review (pp. 67-68)

Ask students these questions:

- What are the differences between the two versions of the miracle of Chanukah? (The version from the Talmud makes no mention of the celebration of Sukot. The story from *II Maccabees* makes no mention of the oil.)

- Which version do you prefer? Why?

- Why did the rabbis ignore the story of Judah Maccabee when they wrote about Chanukah in the Talmud? (The rabbis ignored the story of Judah Maccabee because the account in *II Maccabees* makes no mention of God. The rabbis did not want to draw attention to a story in which God was not responsible for Judah Maccabee's victory over the Greeks.)

- Why didn't the rabbis of later years want Jews to follow the example of Judah Maccabee? (The rabbis of later years didn't want Jews to follow the example of Judah Maccabee because they believed that only God could redeem the Jews from their exile. The rabbis did not believe that Jews fighting in wars without God's help could alter the conditions under which the Jewish people lived.)

Holiday Experience Activities (pp. 69-72)

1. Bring to class books on Jewish ceremonial art so that students can compare different *chanukiot*. There are many books on Jewish ceremonial art, for example, Abram Kanof's *Jewish Ceremonial Art and Religious Observance*. Ask students how the *chanukiot* are different and how they are alike. Have students describe one or two *chanukiot* that they particularly like and explain their choice.

2. Have students create small *chanukiot* out of different lightweight materials, such as construction paper, aluminum foil, pipe cleaners, or Popsicle sticks. When students have finished making their *chanukiot*, ask the rabbi for a space where the *chanukiot* can be exhibited.

3. Every family has its own traditions for making Chanukah special. Ask students what their family does to celebrate Chanukah and what they might add to this year's celebration of the holiday to make it even more special.

Focus on Focus (pp. 73-74)

1. Ask students what assimilation is. Then explain that although assimilation has always been a problem for Jews, Judaism has survived. Ask students to suggest some things Jews in North America can do to keep from assimilating completely.

2.   Although Jewish tradition considers Chanukah a minor holiday, in North America today it is regarded as a major holiday. Have students discuss why this holiday has become so important to us.

Questions to Think About

Throughout history, Jews have suffered because of their beliefs. Ask students: Can you think of anything so precious to you that you would fight or even die for it? Would you be willing to fight or die for Judaism? Have students explain their answers.

Closure

Return to the Opening discussion of the words *freedom* and *assimilation*. Ask students: Now that you have studied this chapter, has your understanding of these words changed? What do the words mean to you now? What do they mean to you as Jews? What do they mean to you as Americans?

Enrichment Activities

1.   Organize a debate or have students conduct a "talk show" with three guests: Moses, Mordecai, and Judah Maccabee. Select three students to play these characters and have each of them state his view on the best way for the Jewish people to attain their freedom. Prepare the students before class by helping them explore their fundamental position:

     "We must have faith and depend on God to save us." (Moses)

     "We have to work within the system, using our political influence." (Mordecai)

     "We have to take up arms and fight for our rights." (Judah Maccabee)

2.   Tell students that Chanukah, like other Jewish holidays, has its own songs. Two traditional songs that can be taught to the class are *Ma'oz Tzur* and *Mi Yemalel?* The words to these songs and their translation appear below. Explore with students what the songs mean. Consider ordering *Haneirot Halalu: A Home Celebration of Chanuka*, a songbook and audiocassette package available from Transcontinental Music Publications, 838 Fifth Avenue, New York, New York 10021.

MA'OZ TZUR
Rock of Ages

Ma'oz tzur yeshuati,   Rock of Ages, let our song
Lecha na'eh leshabe'ach;   Praise Your saving power;

Tikon beit tefilati,	You amid the raging foes,
Vesham todah nezabe'ach.	Were our sheltering tower.
Le'et tachin matbe'ach,	Furious they assailed us,
Mitzar hamenabe'ach,	But Your arm availed us,
Az egmor, beshir mizmor,	And Your word broke their sword
Chanukat hamizbe'ach.	When our own strength failed us.

MI YEMALEL?
Who Can Retell?

Mi yemalel gevurot Yisrael	Who can retell the things that befell us?
Otan mi yimneh?	Who can count them?
Hen bechol dor yakum hagibor	In every age a hero or sage
Go'el ha'am. Shema!	came to our aid. Hark!
Bayamim hahem bazeman hazeh,	At this time of year in days of yore,
Makabi moshi'a ufodeh.	Brave Maccabees led the faithful band.
Uveyameinu kol am Yisrael,	And now the entire nation of Israel must as one arise,
Yitached yakum lehiga'el.	Redeem itself through deed and sacrifice.

3. On Chanukah we eat foods cooked in oil to remember the miracle of the oil. Here is an easy recipe for potato *latkes*.

Potato Latkes

6 potatoes, peeled	3 eggs, beaten
2 medium onions	1/2 tsp. baking powder
1/2 cup matzah meal or flour	salt and pepper to taste
	oil

Grate the potatoes and onions in a food processor. If time permits, set aside this mixture for one hour in a colander with a bowl under it to catch the liquid. Add the matzah meal, eggs, baking powder, salt, and pepper. Heat the oil in a large frying pan. Form pancakes and place them carefully into the pan with a spatula. Fry the pancakes until they are golden and then turn them over. Serve the pancakes topped with sour cream or applesauce.

Resources

Burns, Marilyn. *The Hanukkah Book.* New York: Four Winds Press, 1981.

Frishman, Elyse D. *Haneirot Halalu: These Lights Are Holy.* New York: CCAR Press, 1989.

Grishaver, Joel Lurie. *The True Story of Hanukkah.* Los Angeles: Torah Aura Productions, 1988.

Haneirot Halalv: A Home Celebration of Chanuka (songbook/audiocassette). New York: Transcontinental Music Publications, 1995.

Wolfson, Ron. *The Art of Jewish Living: Hanukah.* New York: Federation of Jewish Mens Clubs, 1990.

Chapter Eight

Tu Bishevat

Chapter Summary

- Tu Bishevat is Hebrew for the fifteenth day of the month of Shevat, which is the New Year for Trees.
- On Tu Bishevat we plant trees if we can and thank God for the bounty of trees and plants that give us food.
- The commandment *Bal Taschit* teaches us that we may not destroy anything that is good and useful.
- Some people celebrate Tu Bishevat with a special *seder*, modeled after the Pesach *seder*.

Instructional Objectives

Students will be able to:

- Describe and explain at least two customs observed on Tu Bishevat.
- Identify at least two of the ways in which Jewish tradition teaches us to care for our environment.
- Explain why the Jewish National Fund was created.

Key Terms

Bal Tashchit	The commandment Do Not Destroy.
Bokser	Carob, a fruit native to Israel that is especially associated with Tu Bishevat.
Chag Ha'ilanot	The Festival of the Trees, another name for Tu Bishevat.

Chag Haperot	The Festival of the Fruit, another name for Tu Bishevat.
Chalutz (pl. Chalutzim)	A pioneer.
Chupah	A wedding canopy.
Eretz Yisrael	The Land of Israel.
Keren Kayemet Leyisrael	The Hebrew name for the Jewish National Fund; literally, the "Fund for the Establishment of Israel."
Kibbutz (pl. Kibbutzim)	A collective settlement in Israel.

Learning Activities

Materials

Food for a Tu Bishevat *seder*; art supplies.

Opening

Most lessons in this teacher's guide assume that students have already read the chapter. This Opening exercise is designed to be done *before* students read the chapter.

Read aloud to students some of the selections that appear on pages 78 and 79 of the textbook. Do not give their sources. Alter any language that reveals the Jewish origins of the selections. For example, read "a scholar" instead of "Rabban Yohanan ben Zakkai." Ask students from where they think the passages come. Ask: What kind of values do they reflect? What kind of people wrote them? When do you think these passages were written?

Ask students if they think these passages come from Jewish tradition. Some students may recognize the Jewish origin of these passages from their religious school education. Ask them if they knew about the Jewish tradition's emphasis on protecting the environment. Explain that this chapter on Tu Bishevat will reveal more about Judaism's attitude toward our environment.

Story Study (pp. 76-77)

Ask students these questions:

- What is the message of the story about the nomad? (The message is that we must partake of and use the natural resources that are available to us without destroying them.)
- What is the message of the *midrash* from *Leviticus Rabbah*? (The message is that we must plant trees and protect the earth for future generations.)

Text Study Review (pp. 78-79)

Ask students the following questions:

- What is the overall message of all seven passages? (Their message is that we must take care of our world, especially the trees and plants because without them we cannot live.)

- Why is planting trees such an important Jewish value? (Planting trees is an important Jewish value because our ancestors recognized that trees give us life, beauty, and sustenance.)

- Of these seven passages, which is your favorite? Why?

- If you wanted to show someone the high value that Judaism places on the environment, which text would you use? Why?

- Today planting a cypress or a cedar tree in honor of a child's birth may not be practical. Why? (There are two problems with planting a cypress or a cedar tree in honor of a child's birth. First, we might not live in an area where those trees grow well or are readily available. Second, because we live in a mobile society, we might not remain in the same area in which we once planted the tree.)

- What might a parent do today to honor the birth of a child? (Parents can plant a tree in Israel in the child's honor. They can also plant a small tree, bush, or flowering bulb that can be uprooted and transplanted if the family moves.)

- What does *Bal Tashchit* mean? (*Bal Tashchit* means "Do Not Destroy." *Bal Tashchit* commands us not to destroy those things that are good and useful, such as our natural resources.)

- What are some of the things we can do to observe the *mitzvah* of *Bal Tashchit*? (We can join local environmental groups, help organize a neighborhood cleanup, make sure that waste in our homes and schools is properly recycled, etc.)

Holiday Experience Activities (p. 80)

1. Since there is no standard text for a Tu Bishevat *seder*, have students go to the library and find books that discuss a Tu Bishevat *seder*. Refer students to Resources on page 56. If they find information about more than one kind of *seder*, have them compare and contrast the *seder*s. If students cannot find books that contain a Tu Bishevat *seder*, ask them what they think such a *seder* should include.

2. Based on the *seder*s they have seen and their own creativity, have students put together their own brief Tu Bishevat *seder*. Have the class agree on the basic structure of the *seder*, and then divide the class into small groups to develop each part. Finally, conduct a Tu Bishevat *seder* with the class. Enlist parents to help, if necessary.

Focus on Focus (pp. 81-82)

1. Have the class (or each student) brainstorm a list of reasons why trees are important. Ask the art teacher to supply materials so students can

create works of art that reflect as many of these reasons as possible. They might make collages, murals, paintings, and so on. Display students' artwork throughout the school.

2. Have students plan a fund-raiser to collect money in order to plant a tree on the grounds of your synagogue or in a nearby park. Have students research the following: the kind of tree that will survive in the climate in which they live, the best time to plant the tree (which in North America may not be near Tu Bishevat), and the kind of care it will need. Make sure that permission to plant the tree is obtained beforehand. Also consider contacting a professional landscaper to advise students on where and how to plant the tree. Meanwhile other students can prepare a planting ceremony that might include prayers, poems, and creative writings about trees.

3. Some of the money that students raise in Activity 2 could also go toward planting trees in Israel. Provide students with information obtained from the Jewish National Fund, which can be contacted at 42 East 69 Street, New York, New York 10021 (212) 879-9300. Ask students whom they would like to honor or memorialize and to explain why.

Exploring Times and Places (pp. 83-84)

Often the *chalutzim* worked with the JNF. Have students go to the library to find out more about the *chalutzim* and the *kibbutzim* and other settlements they established. Ask: Who were the *chalutzim*? What contributions did they make to the Land of Israel? Refer students to Resources below for more information.

Closure

Discuss with students Judaism's high regard for the environment and the world in which we live. Have students summarize these values. Ask: Were you surprised to learn that the Jewish tradition included laws and customs for protecting the environment? What might the rest of the world learn from Judaism in this regard?

Resources

Abrams, Judith Z. *Sukkot: A Family Seder*. Rockville, MD: Kar-Ben Copies, Inc., 1993.
Cone, Molly. *Listen to the Trees: Jews and the Earth*. New York: UAHC Press, 1995.
Fisher, Adam. *Seder Tu Bishevat: The Festival of Trees*. New York: CCAR Press, 1989.

On Chalutzim and Zionism
Elon, Amos. *The Israelis: Founders and Sons*. New York: Bantam Books, 1972.
Hertzberg, Arthur, ed. *The Zionist Idea*. New York: Atheneum, 1981.
Laqueur, Walter. *A History of Zionism*. New York: Schocken Books, 1989.

Chapter Nine

Purim

Chapter Summary

- Purim is celebrated on the fourteenth day of the month of Adar.
- On Purim we read in the Scroll of Esther how Queen Esther and her uncle Mordecai saved the Jews of Persia from the wicked Haman.
- Purim is a fun-filled holiday that we celebrate by eating, drinking, wearing costumes, and distributing gifts.
- Purim reminds us to be aware of our enemies but also to be proud of our Jewish identity.

Instructional Objectives

Students will be able to:

- Relate the story of Queen Esther.
- Describe a *megillah* and tell how it differs from a Torah.
- Explain the connection between anti-Semitism and the holiday of Purim.
- Infer a lesson for today from the Purim story.

Key Terms

Gragger	A noisemaker.
Hamantaschen	Literally, "Haman's hats"; triangular filled pastries traditionally eaten on Purim.

58

Megillah	A scroll; on Purim we read the Scroll of Esther.
Mcgillat Esthcr	Thc Scroll of Esther.
Purimspiel	A humorous Purim play.
Shalach Manot	Literally, "Sending Portions"; gifts of tasty food sent to friends and the poor on Purim; also referred to as *Mishlo'ach Manot.*
Shushan Purim	The fifteenth of Adar, when Purim is observed in walled cities.

Learning Activities

Materials

Art supplies for making *megillot;* markers and poster board.

Opening

Ask students if they can recall a time when they took a big risk by standing up for something in which they believed–something really important to them–even though doing so might have meant their getting into trouble or losing a friend.

Explain that Queen Esther did just that in the Purim story: She risked disobeying the king's rules in order to save the Jewish people.

Story Study (pp. 86-89)

Ask students the following questions:

- Who are the main characters in the Purim story? (The main characters are King Ahasuerus of Persia; his second wife, Queen Esther; her uncle, Mordecai; and Ahasuerus's prime minister, Haman.)

- What do you think of the fact that Esther kept her Jewish identity a secret? Do you think she was right to do so?

- Why did Mordecai refuse to bow down to Haman? (Mordecai refused to bow down to Haman because he was a Jew, and Jews are forbidden by the Second Commandment to bow down to anyone other than God. Suggest that students turn to page 137 for the text of the Second Commandment.)

- Does the story contain any clues that show the Jews' laws were "different from those of everyone else" and that the Jews did "not obey the king's laws"? Why do you think Haman wanted to destroy the Jews? (The most obvious clue in the story is Mordecai's refusal to bow down to Haman. Haman wanted to destroy the Jews because they refused to pay him homage. He resented the fact that the Jews placed their God before him and refused to change their beliefs and practices to fulfill Haman's lust for power.)

- How did Esther save the Jews? (by revealing to Ahasuerus that she was Jewish and that if Haman's edict to destroy the Jews was carried out, she, too, would be killed)

- According to the text, how are we supposed to celebrate the fourteenth day of Adar? (On the fourteenth day of Adar, we are supposed to feast and make merry. It is a tradition to hold a masquerade party in which many of the participants dress up as characters in the story of Esther. We also give presents, which we call *Shalach Manot*, to our friends and the poor.)

Text Study Review (p. 90)

Ask students the following questions:

- Some people think that the last two lines of the Torah text are contradictory: On the one hand, we are told to "blot out the memory of Amalek," but then we are reminded not to forget. How is it possible to "blot out the memory" and "not forget" at the same time? What do you think this verse means? (This is a difficult verse to understand. There are several possible interpretations: One is that we are not to forget *until* we have blotted out the memory of Amalek; only then are we allowed to forget. Another is that we are asked to remember *and* to blot out the memory of Amalek because it is important to do both. We must forever struggle to remove from memory those who did evil because that is the only way to prevent evil from happening again.)

- Why do you think this Torah portion is read on the Shabbat before Purim? Why do you think the Shabbat before Purim is called *Shabbat Zachor, Zachor* meaning "Remember"? (In general, the idea of memory is very important to the Jewish people because of our history of suffering. On this Shabbat, Jews are reminded of the cowardly attack of the Amalekites on our people not only by this passage but also by the connection between the Amalekites and Haman, a descendant of the Amalekite king Agog.)

- Why do you think Moses warned the Israelites about Amalek as they prepared to enter the Promised Land? (Moses did not want the Jews to be overconfident and thus unprepared when they entered the Promised Land, which at that time contained many tribes who would be hostile to the Jews.)

- The text states that the name Amalek is a symbol for evil in the world. History shows that throughout the ages, Amalek has arisen to destroy us. Ask the class to name some other "Amaleks" in Jewish history. (There were many "Amaleks" in Jewish history. Among the most prominent were the Romans, the leaders of the Spanish Inquisition, the Russian cossacks, and the Nazis.)

Holiday Experience Activities (pp. 91-92)

1. Ask students these questions:

    *   What does the word *megillah* mean? (*Megillah* means "scroll.")

    *   Why is *Megillat Esther* unusual? (*Megillat Esther* is unique because it does not mention God's name even once.)

2. There are actually five *megillot*, and each one is read on a different Jewish holiday. Have students go to the library, look up the names of the other four *megillot*, and note on which holiday each one is read. (The other four *megillot* are the Song of Songs, the Book of Ruth, the Book of Ecclesiastes, and the Book of Lamentations. The Song of Songs is read on Passover, the Book of Ruth on Sukot, the Book of Ecclesiastes on Shavuot, and the Book of Lamentations on Tishah Be'av.)

3. Gather together various art supplies, such as construction paper, glue or tape, wooden dowels, ribbon, markers or paint, and glitter. Divide students into small groups and have each group design a series of pictures that tell Esther's story. When the groups are done, have each group tape or glue its pictures together in one long row that resembles a scroll. Instruct the groups to tape or glue one end of their "scroll" to a dowel. Then have each group roll up its Scroll of Esther and tie it with ribbon so that the paper can curl. At a later time, have each group present its *Megillat Esther* to the rest of the class.

4. Arrange to use the synagogue kitchen. After discussing with the class what the practice of *Shaloch Manot* is, take students to the kitchen and bake *hamantaschen* with them. A recipe for *hamantaschen* appears in Enrichment Activity 3. After the *hamantaschen* have been baked and cooled, discuss with the class to whom they wish to send these pastries. To their parents? To their friends? To a homeless shelter? To a nursing home? To a local hospital? Have the class reach a consensus. If students decide on one of the latter three choices, prepare a holiday card for each student to sign.

Focus on Focus (p. 93)

1. Provide students with markers and poster board and have each of them create a Wanted sign for Haman. Ask them to imagine what Haman looked like and to draw his face on the sign. Next to it they should include facts about Haman, some of which they can make up (e.g., hair color, eye color, height, weight) and some of which they can elicit from Esther's story (e.g., "Wanted for plotting the murder of Jews" or "Wanted for threatening the life of the queen").

2. Have students interview a parent, adult relative, or family friend who has experienced prejudice. Suggest that students ask the person the following questions:

- What happened?

- How did you feel about what happened?

- How did you respond to what happened?

- Why did you respond that way?

Questions to Think About

Have students give some thought to what makes a person a hero. Ask: Were Esther and Mordecai heroes? Why or why not? Can someone be a good role model without being a hero? Were Esther and Mordecai good role models? Have students explain their answers.

Closure

Return to the issue raised in the Opening section. Ask students what taking a risk for what one believes has to do with Purim. Ask: Why is standing up for what one believes an important Jewish value?

Enrichment Activities

1. Have students write a *Purimspiel*. Tell them that in a "traditional" *Purimspiel*, the actors make fun of teachers, rabbis, parents, and Jewish leaders. The *Purimspiel* may even be a retelling of the Purim story in the style of a popular movie or TV show. Invite parents or other classes to watch the class's *Purimspiel*.

2. Another common Purim activity is the Purim carnival, which consists of games and other activities for the participants. Plan a small Purim carnival with the class. Encourage pairs of students to develop simple games or activities and then invite the other students in the class or students in other classes to participate in them. Fun and simple games can include a ringtoss or a wheel of fortune.

3. Bake *hamantaschen*, triangular filled pastries, with the class.

Joyce's Hamantaschen

Dough
1¼ cups butter
1 cup sugar
2 eggs
1 tsp. vanilla
5 tbsps. water
4 cups sifted flour

Filling
Any store-bought filling: poppy seed, prune, apricot, etc., in a can or jar.

Preheat the oven to 375°F. Cream the butter and sugar. Add the eggs, creaming until the mixture is smooth. Add the water and vanilla and then the flour and mix until the dough forms a ball. Wrap the ball in plastic wrap and refrigerate for a few hours. Divide the dough into sections. Roll each section of the dough out on a floured board until it is ¼″ thick. Cut out circles, using the open end of a glass. Experiment with different glasses until you find a size you like. You can make big *hamantaschen* or little ones. Put a spoonful of the filling in the center of each circle and lift the edges to form a triangle. Bake on a greased cookie sheet for 15 minutes. Makes about 5 dozen *hamantaschen*, depending on the size of the circles.

Resources

Diamant, Anita. *Living a Jewish Life.* New York: HarperCollins, 1991.

Goodman, Philip. *The Purim Anthology.* Philadelphia: The Jewish Publication Society, 1988.

Chapter Ten

Pesach

Chapter Summary

- Pesach, one of the *Shalosh Regalim*, is observed for seven days, beginning on the fifteenth of Nisan.

- Pesach is also called *Zeman Cherutenu*, the "Season of our Freedom," because on this holiday we celebrate the Exodus from Egypt, when God freed the Israelites from slavery in Egypt.

- On the first night of Pesach, we participate in a *seder*, a ritual meal during which we use a *haggadah* to tell the story of the Exodus from Egypt.

- During the *seder* we eat certain symbolic foods, including *matzah* and *maror*, bitter herbs.

- We eat *matzah* instead of bread during Pesach; during the whole week of Pesach, we refrain from eating leavened bread and anything made from wheat, rye, barley, oats, or spelt.

- We keep track of the fifty days between Pesach and Shavuot by *Sefirat Ha'Omer*, "Counting the *Omer*."

Instructional Objectives

Students will be able to:

- Tell what happened on the night God sent the tenth plague against the Egyptians.

- Identify the symbolic foods that we eat during the *seder* and explain their meaning.

- Explain the symbolic meaning of *matzah*.

- Conduct a traditional *bedikat chametz*, search for *chametz*.
- Identify what *chametz* and the different types of *chametz* are.

Key Terms

Bedikat chametz	The symbolic search for *chametz*.
Betzah	A roasted egg.
Chametz	Leavened bread and anything made from wheat, rye, barley, oats, or spelt; refers to prohibited foods during Pesach.
Charoset	A mixture of fruit, nuts, and wine.
Haggadah	The book that contains the liturgy for the *seder*.
Karpas	Parsley or other greens.
Lag Ba'omer	The thirty-third day of the counting of the *Omer*, celebrated as a minor holiday.
Lechem oni	Literally, the "bread of affliction"; *matzah*.
Maror	Bitter herbs.
Matzah	Unleavened bread.
Rachamim	Mercy, kindness.
Seder (pl. Sedarim)	Literally, "order"; a ritual meal in which we participate on the first night of Pesach.
Sefirat Ha'Omer	Literally, "Counting the *Omer*"; the fifty days between Pesach and Shavuot.
Zeman Cherutenu	The Season of Our Freedom, another name for Pesach.
Zeroa	A roasted shankbone.

Learning Activities

Materials

Bibles; *siddurim*; index cards for making flash cards, oaktag; *seder* plates, books on Jewish ceremonial art, art supplies for making *seder* plates; copies of *Pirkei Avot*, additional art supplies; flour, water, sugar, a packet of yeast, and two bowls; dried beans, peas, and two or three bowls; different editions of *haggadot*.

Opening

Ask students which Jewish holiday they think is observed by more North American Jews than any other. (According to statistics, one out of every ten Jews lights Shabbat candles; one half of all Jews fast on Yom Kippur; and nine out of ten Jews observe Pesach in some way.) Ask students why they think Pesach is the most commonly observed holiday.

One reason for the popularity of Pesach is its message of redemption from slavery. Ask students why this is such a significant concept for Jews. (Although the majority of Jews today live in Israel and North America where we are free to be Jews, we remember that throughout our history, people have tried to enslave the Jews. In modern times, we have survived the Holocaust, oppression in the former Soviet Union, and attacks from hostile Arab nations. We know what going from slavery to freedom means.)

Story Study (pp. 96-97)

1.   Ask students the following questions:

   •   What preparations did the Israelites have to make before the last plague? (The Israelite families were instructed by Moses to slaughter lambs for the passover offering, dip sprigs of hyssop [a plant used in ancient times for certain rituals] in the lambs' blood, and brush the blood on the lintel and the two doorposts.)

   •   From where does the tradition of eating *matzah* on Pesach come? (On the morning after the last plague, the Israelites left Egypt before the bread that they had prepared for baking had time to rise. So they baked the unleavened bread and took it with them.)

2.   Have students look up the first nine plagues in the Book of Exodus, 7:14-10:29. Ask them to list the first nine plagues and what Pharaoh did after each plague. (The nine plagues and the passages in Exodus in which they are first mentioned appear in the following order: blood–7:19; frogs–7:27; lice–8:12; insect swarms–8:17; pestilence–9:3; boils–9:9; hail–9:18; locusts–10:4; and darkness–10:21.)

Text Study Review (pp. 98-99)

1.   Distribute *siddurim* to students. Have them look through the prayer book and make a list of the ways in which God is portrayed in the liturgy. You might choose to have students do this exercise in pairs. Have students look in particular at such parts of the service as *Ma'ariv Aravim, Ahavat Olam,* and *Hashkivenu.*

2.   Ask students:

   •   How is God portrayed in the "Song at the Sea?" (God is portrayed as a Warrior, who is to be feared and respected.)

   •   Is this a different image of God from the one we would expect? How is this portrayal of God different from or similar to how God is portrayed in the siddur?

3.   The parting of the Sea of Reeds is called a miracle. Ask students the following questions:

- What are some other miracles that occur in the Torah? (There are many miracles in the Torah. One small miracle is the burning bush through which God spoke to Moses; another is the manna that God sent to the Israelites in the wilderness.)

- Do you believe that these miracles really happened? Why or why not?

- Do you believe that miracles happen today? Why or why not?

4. Ask students to give a definition of *rachamim*. Have them describe how they think a *rachaman*, someone who is full of *rachamim*, should behave.

Holiday Experience Activities (pp. 100-103)

1. Ask students to imagine what the *seder* would be like if there were no *seder*, meaning "order," to the ritual and we had to decide for ourselves how to tell the story of the Exodus from Egypt. Explore the meaning of order with students by having them experience disorder. Have the class conduct a "mixed-up" model *seder* in which the parts of the *seder* are done in random order. For example, write the names of the parts of the *seder* on small pieces of paper, fold up the pieces, and have students draw them from a hat. After students have conducted the mixed-up model *seder*, have them compare it to a *seder* that follows the traditional order. Ask them how the traditional order helps them follow the story and learn the meaning of Pesach.

2. Have students design flash cards, one for each part of the *seder*. Instruct students to use the cards to learn about the *seder* ritual and the order in which the parts of the *seder* are performed. Encourage students to embellish their cards in creative ways and, once they know the order of the *seder*, to paste them one after the other on a sheet of oaktag, which they can then take home.

3. Show students a *seder* plate. If possible, show them more than one such plate or have them look at photographs of *seder* plates in books on Jewish ceremonial art. With the help of the art teacher, have students make *seder* plates to hold the symbolic foods used during the *seder*.

4. Ask students the following questions:
   - What is the significance of each of the symbolic foods of the *seder*: *zeroa*, *betzah*, *matzah*, *maror*, *karpas*, and *charoset*? (The *zeroa*–shankbone–recalls the slaughtered paschal lamb whose blood was painted on the lintel and doorposts and led God to pass over the homes of the Israelites. The *betzah*–roasted egg–is a reminder of the Temple sacrifices and the second lamb offered on festival days. The *matzah* symbolizes the unleavened bread that the Jews ate as they hurried out of Egypt. The *maror*–bitter herbs–recalls the bitterness of our ancestors' slavery. The *karpas*–leafy greens–dipped in salt

water signifies both the coming of spring and the salty tears that our ancestors wept during their slavery. The *karpas* is eaten with *charoset*, which is a mixture of fruits, nuts, and wine that symbolizes the mortar used for the bricks the Israelites had to make as slaves.)

- How are the four cups of wine at the *seder* related to the theme of redemption? (Each cup of wine symbolizes one aspect of God's redemption of the Israelites: God "freed" us, "saved" us, "redeemed" us, and "took" us to be God's people.)

- Who is Elijah? (Elijah was a prophet who lived during the reign of King Ahab. He was a stern and fearless prophet, best remembered for his deadly confrontation with the priests of Baal on Mount Carmel. Elijah was later linked in Jewish tradition to the coming of the Messiah.)

- Why do we put a cup of wine on the *seder* table for Elijah? (According to Jewish tradition, Elijah will announce the coming of the Messiah. The cup for Elijah symbolizes our hope that the peace the Messiah will bring comes soon.)

- Are there really *four* questions? (There is actually only one question, and that question is, "How is this night different from all other nights?" There are, however, four answers to that question. The confusion has arisen in part from the fact that in some *haggadot*, the question is printed four times.)

- Who says the Four Questions in your family?

Family Album Focus (p. 104)

Discuss the answers to the following questions with the class:

- Which "spring cleaning" chores must be done in order to prepare for Pesach? (Families are supposed to remove all *chametz* from the house before Pesach arrives. Then each family should check the house for stray crumbs, a procedure that is called *bedikat chametz*. On the night before Pesach, all remaining *chametz* should be removed from the house and burned.)

- What does your family do to prepare for Pesach?

Focus on Focus (pp. 105-106)

1. Ask students what the meaning of *matzah* is according to the excerpt from the *haggadah* on page 105 of the textbook. (The *haggadah* calls *matzah* the bread of affliction because it was the bread that the Israelites ate in the land of Egypt.)

2. The *seder* ritual is supposed to inspire us to help those who are less fortunate than we are. Ask students to think of another holiday that encourages us to think of the welfare of others. Have them explain their

68

answer. (On Yom Kippur, we are supposed to think of the poor and the needy as we contemplate our own sins; on Purim, we give *Shalach Manot* not only to our friends and relatives but to the indigent and helpless.)

3. Ask students:

    *   What makes food *chametz*? (Food is *chametz* if it is made from one of five grains that have been leavened by yeast.)

    *   What is the rule that keeps *matzah* for Pesach from becoming *chametz*? (Once flour is mixed with water, the doughy mixture must be prepared within the next eighteen minutes so that it does not rise and become *chametz*.)

4. Have students list some of the foods considered *chametz* by certain groups of Jews and not considered *chametz* by others. Ask students why these foods are controversial and if their family eats them.

5. Have pairs of students decide which of the following foods are *Kascher lePesach*, "kosher for Passover." If students are not sure, tell them to go to the supermarket or their own kitchen to read the labels. The controversial foods (rice, legumes, corn) are called *kitniyot*. Have students mark each item on the list below as follows: K if it is *Kascher lePesach*, KK if it is *Kascher lePesach* but contains *kitniyot*, and C if it is *chametz*.

yogurt	K	crackers	C
rye bread	C	celery	K
apples	K	beer	C
apple pie	C	instant oatmeal	C
milk	K	corn flakes	C
jelly	K	peanut butter	KK
macaroni and cheese	C	mayonnaise	K
flour	C	frozen pizza	C
pretzels	C	tortilla chips	KK
American cheese	K	soy sauce	KK

Exploring Times and Places (p. 107)

During the *Omer*, it is customary to read from *Pirkei Avot*, the "Sayings of the Fathers," a book of the Talmud that contains the wisdom of the ancient rabbis in a very readable, understandable form. We honor the memory of these rabbis on Lag Ba'omer. Some of the rabbis taught the importance of good deeds; others emphasized the importance of learning Torah. Have students look at *Pirkei Avot* and ask them to choose a favorite saying. There are many editions of *Pirkei Avot* available. Sections of *Pirkei Avot* are also reproduced in *Gates of Prayer*, pages 16-28. Have students use the saying they chose as the basis for a piece of art. They could illustrate the saying, interpret it, or illuminate the text. Ask the art teacher to help with this activity.

Closure

Ask students what they learned in this chapter that might make their next *seder* more meaningful. Ask them how this knowledge might help them participate more fully in the Pesach experience.

Enrichment Activities

1. Do the following scientific experiments with students to help them understand how the yeast fungus works and why the question of legumes came up in the first place.

    a. Make two batches of dough. For the first, combine three cups of flour, one cup of warm water, and one tablespoon of sugar in a bowl. For the second, mix one cup of warm water and one tablespoon of sugar with a packet of yeast in another bowl and then add three cups of flour to this mixture. Put both batches of dough in a warm place. Have students observe and record what happened to each one.

    b. Bring in two or three varieties of dried beans and peas. Put half a cup of each type of legume in a bowl with three cups of water. Let the soaked legumes stand for several hours and then measure the volume of the beans and peas. Have students describe what they observed.

2. The *haggadah* holds an important place in Jewish tradition. The first *haggadot* were written about two thousand years ago. All *haggadot* contain the same elements and follow the same order: They all tell the story of the Exodus from Egypt and they all incorporate the symbolic foods of the Pesach *seder*. However, there are more editions of the *haggadah* than of any other Jewish text. Have students look at several different *haggadot*. Ask them how they are similar and how they are different. Have students look at the same part of the *seder* in each of these *haggadot*. Ask them to describe how the illustrations and texts differ. See Resources on page 71 for a list of *haggadot*.

3. In one section of the *haggadah,* four different types of children are described. The four types of children can be viewed as symbols of four approaches to Jewish life. Have students look at this passage in a *haggadah* and identify the four types of children. Ask students how each child approaches the Pesach holiday. Ask: What do we tell each one? What kind of person does each child represent? (The four types of children are the wise child, the wicked child, the simple child, and the child who does not know to ask. The wise child's approach to the holiday is that of a

scholar: That child wishes to know more about the holiday and how to observe it. The wicked child's approach is that of a rebel: That child does not wish to be counted among those who were saved from slavery by God's might. The simple child's approach is that of one who does not understand what is going on: That child wishes to know what the holiday is about. The child who cannot ask is usually the youngest child at a *seder*: That child does not even know enough to ask and so must be told about the holiday. To the wise child, we explain the observances of the holiday; to the wicked child, we make clear that the effect of separating oneself from the community results in estrangement from that community; to the simple child, we explain God's might; and to the child who does not know to ask, we tell the story of Passover.)

4. If possible, make the following Pesach foods with the class, using the recipes below.

Charoset

1 apple	1/2 tsp. cinnamon
1/2 cup chopped nuts	Grated rind of 1 lemon
2 tsps. sugar or honey	1 tbsp. sweet red wine or grape juice

Peel the apple and chop it coarsely. Then combine all the ingredients. Add more sugar, cinnamon, and wine as desired.

Matzah Brei

4 pieces of *matzah*
3 eggs
Margarine, butter, or other fat for frying
Salt and pepper, if desired

Break the *matzah* into a bowl. Fill the bowl with hot water to cover the *matzah* and then drain immediately. Squeeze out as much water as possible. In another bowl, break the eggs and beat well. Add the eggs to the *matzah* and toss together. Melt margarine in a large frying pan over medium heat. Add the *matzah* mixture and cook until it is done. You can cook one side of the mixture completely and then turn it like a pancake, or you can scramble the mixture during cooking until it is done. Serve hot with salt and pepper, sugar, or syrup. (Serves 3-4)

Resources

Steingroot, Ira. *Keeping Passover*. New York: HarperCollins, 1995.

Wolfson, Ron. *The Art of Jewish Living: The Passover Seder*. New York: Federation of Jewish Mens Clubs, 1988.

Various Haggadot

Bronstein, Herbert, ed. *A Passover Haggadah.* New York: CCAR Press, 1975.

Levy, Richard N., ed. *On Wings of Freedom.* Hoboken, NJ: Ktav, 1989.

Rabinowicz, Rachel Anne, ed. *Passover Haggadah: The Feast of Freedom.* New York: The Rabbinical Assembly, 1982.

Silberman, Shoshana. *A Family Haggadah.* Rockville, MD: Kar-Ben Copies, Inc., 1987.

Simon, Chanan. *The Why Haggadah.* Woodmere, NY: Beit-Shamai Publications, Inc., 1989.

Wiesel, Elie. *A Passover Haggadah.* New York: Simon & Schuster, Inc., 1993.

Chapter Eleven

Yom Hashoah

Chapter Summary

- Yom Hashoah is Holocaust Memorial Day, which is observed on the twenty-seventh of Nisan.

- On Yom Hashoah we mourn those who were murdered by the Nazis during World War II.

- Many Jews commemorate Yom Hashoah by lighting six candles to remember the six million Jews who died in the Holocaust and by gathering for special services that include prayers, poems, and solemn observances.

- Yom Hashoah helps Jews remember the Holocaust so that such inhumanity never happens again.

Instructional Objectives

Students will be able to:

- Explain why it is important to remember the victims of the Holocaust.

- Describe some of the ways in which Yom Hashoah is observed.

Key Terms

Chasidei Umot Ha'olam   Literally, the "Pious Ones of the Nations of the World"; the Righteous Gentiles who Jsaved Jews during the Holocaust.

74

Shoah   Literally, "destruction" or "catastrophe"; the
                               Holocaust.

Yahrzeit   The anniversary of a death.

Learning Activities

Materials

... *I never saw another butterfly* ... (see Resource on page 76).

Opening

Show students the drawings in the book ...*I never saw another butterfly*...without telling them anything about the artists. Ask students what they think the drawings are about. Then have them imagine the artists' lives.

Tell students that they are going to spend some time talking about the Holocaust. Point out that the Holocaust did not affect only adults. Of the six million Jews who were killed in the Holocaust, one and a half million were children.

Story Study (pp. 110-112)

Ask students the following questions:

- How did Menachem feel about waiting and why? (Menachem both liked and disliked waiting. He liked waiting because it meant that he was still alive; he disliked it because waiting reminded him of how hungry he was.)

- How do you think Menachem felt when he saw the German command car coming up the street? (Menachem probably felt excited and scared–excited at the opportunity to do something important and dangerous and scared that he might be killed doing it.)

- Why do you think Mike never talked about his experiences in the Warsaw Ghetto? (Mike never spoke about his experiences because of the painful memories of his family's death and his own suffering in the Warsaw Ghetto.)

- How do you think Mike answered the question "Daddy, were you ever a slave?"

- How would you answer the same question?

Text Study Review (pp. 113-115)

1. Have students read the three texts carefully. Ask them to write a paragraph or two describing their emotional responses to the diary entry and two poems. In addition, encourage students to discuss other material they have read about the Holocaust.

2. Discuss the following questions with students:

- Anne Frank says that it's really a wonder she was able to maintain her beliefs in the face of confusion, misery, and death. How do you think other Jews managed to keep their faith while hiding in cellars and suffering in concentration camps?

- What did Martin Niemoller learn from his experience during the Holocaust? (Niemoller learned that we must speak out against injustice no matter when it happens, regardless of whom it affects. If we don't speak out early, it becomes more difficult to stop injustice later.)

Holiday Experience Activity (p. 116)

Using the information presented on page 116, including the ideas contained in the captions, have the class create its own Yom Hashoah observance. Invite other classes, even the whole school, and parents to attend. Consider dividing the class into small groups for this project and having each group plan a part of the observance. Encourage students to go to the library and search for information, readings, and ideas.

Focus on Focus (pp. 117-118)

1. Ask students to spend a few days reading newspapers or news magazines at home. Then pose the following questions about what they read:

   - Where in the world today are there people who are suffering from oppression?

   - What is our country doing to help them?

   - What could we, as individuals, do to help them?

   - Are there any lessons from the Holocaust that we can apply to these situations? What are they?

2. Have the class plan a fund-raiser or another *tzedakah* project to benefit one of the groups of people discussed in the previous activity who are suffering from oppression today.

3. Ask students the following questions:

   - What can we do to teach the lessons of the Holocaust and insure that people never forget? (We can read books, show films, conduct slide shows, organize art exhibits, and teach about the Holocaust in our schools and homes.)

   - Which word do you prefer to use for what happened to the Jews during World War II, *Shoah* or Holocaust? Why?

Closure

Ask students if they think the 614th *mitzvah* (discussed on page 118) is important. Ask: Do you observe the 614th *mitzvah*? How?

Resource

Volavkova, Hana, ed. *... I never saw another butterfly...: Children's Drawings and Poems from Terezın, 1942-1944.* New York: McGraw-Hill Book Co., 1976.

Chapter Twelve

Yom Ha'atzmaut

Chapter Summary

- Yom Ha'atzmaut, Israel Independence Day, is celebrated on the fifth of Iyar.

- The modern State of Israel declared its independence in 1948.

- In Israel, the day before Yom Ha'atzmaut is Yom Hazikaron, Memorial Day, for those soldiers who died defending the State of Israel.

- Yom Ha'atzmaut is celebrated with parades, fireworks, and festivals.

- God promised the Land of Israel to Abraham and his descendants in the Book of Genesis. Ever since then, Jews have loved and longed for the Land of Israel.

- In 1897, Theodor Herzl organized an international movement called Zionism that fostered the idea of a Jewish state. Although Herzl died in 1904, his dream lived on.

- The modern democratic State of Israel is the fulfillment of that dream.

Instructional Objectives

Students will be able to:

- Discuss the events that motivated Theodor Herzl to organize the Zionist movement.

- Explain why some Jews have a strong emotional connection to the Land of Israel.

- List some of the activities that might be organized in celebration of Yom Ha'atzmaut.

Key Terms

Aliyah

Literally, "going up"; refers both to immigrating to Israel and to the honor of being called up to the *bimah* to recite or chant the blessings over the Torah.

Eretz Yisrael

The Land of Israel.

Hatikvah

Literally, "The Hope"; the name of Israel's national anthem.

Yom Hazikaron

Memorial Day for soldiers who died defending the State of Israel.

Yom Yerushalayim

Jerusalem Day, celebrated on the twenty-eighth of Iyar.

Zionist

One who loves and supports Israel.

Learning Activities

Materials

A recording of *Hatikvah*; paper and drawing supplies.

Opening

Have students read the quote on page 119 and then rephrase Ben-Gurion's statement. Ask: What was Ben-Gurion saying? What feelings was he expressing?

Ask students if they can imagine something being so important to them that they would be willing to "offer up" their life for it.

Story Study (pp. 120-122)

Ask students the following questions:

- What events changed Theodor Herzl's life forever and made him pay attention to his Jewish heritage at the age of thirty-five? (Herzl's life changed after he attended the trial of French army captain Alfred Dreyfus, who had been accused of spying. Although many thought that Dreyfus was innocent, he was found guilty and was stripped of his military honors. What shocked Herzl the most was the anti-Semitic sentiment of many of the French citizens.)

- Why did Herzl decide that the Jews needed a state of their own? (The Dreyfus Affair made Herzl realize that Jews would never be completely accepted by the countries in which they already lived, no matter how well they seemed to fit into the country's culture. To live in complete freedom without fear of prejudice and persecution, Jews had to have their own country.)

- What happened at the First Zionist Congress? (At the First Zionist

Congress, those Jewish leaders from around the world whom Herzl had invited formed an official organization, created a flag, and began raising funds for the founding of a Jewish state.)

- What was Herzl's attitude toward the founding of a Jewish state? (Although Herzl thought founding a Jewish state was absolutely necessary for the security of the Jews, he also realized that the road ahead would be long and difficult. Undeterred, Herzl spent the remaining years of his life working to realize his goal of founding a Jewish state.)

- What did Herzl mean by the statement "If you will it, it is not a dream"? (This is one of the most famous statements in modern Jewish history. Herzl knew that there would be no Jewish state if Jews did not take an active role in founding it.)

- Did Herzl's dream come true? How and when? (Herzl's dream came true on May 14, 1948, when David Ben-Gurion declared Israel an independent nation.)

Text Study Review (pp. 123-125)

1. Ask students the following questions:

   - Israel is often called the Promised Land because of the promises that God made to Abraham, Isaac, and Jacob. What exactly does God promise to Abraham in the passage from Genesis 12 and to Isaac in Genesis 26? (God promises Abraham to make his descendants a great nation. God promises the same to Isaac but adds that he will give Isaac's descendants all of the land in which Isaac and his family live.)

   - Why do you think that Israel is still called the Promised Land?

   - What does the Psalmist say will happen if he forgets Jerusalem? What do you think the poet was trying to say? Why? (When the Psalmist says, "If I forget you, O Jerusalem,/ Let my right hand forget her cunning./ … let my tongue stick to the roof of my mouth," he is saying that if he forgets Jerusalem, may he lose his intelligence and become silent.)

   - What does Judah Halevi say about his life in his poem? (Judah Halevi sees his life in Spain as empty and without sustenance–his food has no flavor and he has no appetite–because he is far from Jerusalem and Jerusalem is under foreign rule.)

2. Judah Halevi was not alone in writing about Israel. Throughout our history, Jews have written of their yearning to return to the Land of Israel. Have students go to the library and find another example of such writing. Ask them to note the name of the author and some information about him or her and then write a few sentences summarizing the work they chose.

3. Play a recording of *Hatikvah* for students. Ask them to write down or draw their reactions to Israel's national anthem. If possible, invite the music teacher or the cantor to teach *Hatikvah* to the students.

Holiday Experience Activity (p. 126)

If there are plans to celebrate Yom Ha'atzmaut in your community, have students find out what roles they can play in arranging and participating in the celebration. If there are no such plans, have students organize a class celebration of the holiday. Have them decorate the classroom and hold a small party, at which time they may view a short film about Israel or listen to someone speak about living in Israel. Encourage students to make Israeli food at home to bring to class and serve.

Focus on Focus (p. 128)

1. Ask students to interview relatives or other adults who have been to Israel. Suggest that students pose the following questions to the adults they interview:

    * When did you first go to Israel?

    * How did you feel about Israel after that first visit?

    * When was the last time you were in Israel?

    * How do you feel about Israel now?

If any of the students have been to Israel, you might ask them to bring in photographs, show slides, etc.

2. Have students brainstorm a list of the ways in which people who do not live in Israel can show their support for it. Then have the class vote on a way to do something in support of Israel and do it. Consider contacting the local Jewish Federation and asking it to send a United Jewish Appeal representative to discuss the ways in which your Jewish community can express its support for Israel.

Exploring Times and Places (pp. 129-130)

1. Have students interview individuals who remember what happened at the United Nations on November 29, 1947. Make sure they ask the interviewees how they felt while waiting for the vote to be completed and what the interviewees remember about the reaction to the vote.

2. Have students reenact the events that occurred on November 29, 1947. Assign the following parts to students: Jews sitting by their radio; the head of the Security Council who called each country by name; representatives of various nations such as the United States, the Soviet Union, France, England, Jordan; Jews celebrating the outcome of the vote. Have students do any necessary research in the library. Refer them to Resources on the next page. Have students perform their skit for another class or their parents, perhaps as part of a Yom Ha'atzmaut celebration.

Closure

Conclude by asking students to make a list of the things they know about Israel. You could choose to work together as a class to compile one list on the chalkboard. Have students discuss what the list reflects about their feelings about Israel.

Enrichment Activity

Israeli food is food that is eaten in most Middle Eastern countries. Two typical Israeli foods are hummus and techina. Hummus is made from ground chickpeas. Techina is made from ground sesame seeds. Mixed together with some seasoning, they make a delicious and healthy dip. Consider arranging with your local temple for use of its kitchen to prepare hummus, which includes techina, with students.

Hummus

2 16-oz. cans chickpeas

1 or 2 cloves garlic, peeled
1 tbsp. lemon juice
1 11-oz. can techina (1 1/2 cups), sometimes called tehini (or put 1/2 cup toasted sesame seeds and 1 cup water in a blender and puree until smooth)

a handful of toasted pine nuts (optional)
paprika
pita bread
olive oil

Drain the chickpeas. Puree them in a food processor until they are crushed well. Add the garlic cloves to the paste and process again. Then add the lemon juice and techina. Process the mixture until it is smooth. Place it in a wide, shallow bowl. Smooth the top with a spatula. Cover the mixture with a thin coat of olive oil. Sprinkle with toasted pine nuts (if desired) and paprika. Serve with pita bread sliced into eighths.

Resources

Friedman, Thomas. *From Beirut to Jerusalem*. Garden City, NY: Doubleday, 1990.

Hertzberg, Arthur. *The Zionist Idea*. New York: Atheneum, 1981.

Laqueur, Walter. *A History of Zionism*. New York: Schocken Books, 1989.

Shipler, David. *Arab and Jew: Wounded Spirits in a Promised Land*. New York: Penguin Books, 1987.

Chapter Thirteen

Shavuot

Chapter Summary

- Shavuot, which is celebrated on the sixth of Sivan, is called *Zeman Matan Toratenu*, the "Time of the Giving of Our Torah."

- On Shavuot we praise God for giving us the Torah.

- Shavuot is also *Chag Habikurim*, the "Festival of the First Fruits"; in Israel, the first summer fruits are harvested on Shavuot.

- The Torah portion for Shavuot includes the reading of the Ten Commandments.

- When we read the Ten Commandments on Shavuot, we reaffirm the *berit*, the "covenant," between God and the Jewish people.

- Many synagogues hold the ceremony of confirmation on Shavuot.

Instructional Objectives

Students will be able to:

- List the Ten Commandments.

- Explain the history of confirmation and name at least one component of the confirmation ceremony.

- Analyze the different views of revelation and give their own opinion about what the Israelites heard at Mount Sinai.

Key Terms

Am Berit	A Covenant People; refers to the Jews.
Aseret Hadibrot	The Ten Commandments.

Bar mitzvah	Literally, "son of the commandment"; a ceremony marking a Jewish boy's reaching the age of thirteen, when he is responsible for the performance of *mitzvot*.
Berit	The covenant.
Bet midrash	A house of study.
Chag Habikurim	The Festival of the First Fruits, another name for Shavuot.
Ketuvim	Writings; the third section of the Bible.
Nevi'im	Prophets; the second section of the Bible.
Parashah (pl. Parashiyot)	The weekly Torah portion.
Tanach	The three sections of the Hebrew Bible consisting of Torah, Prophets, and Writings.
Tikun Leil Shavuot	The custom of studying Torah late into the night on Shavuot.
Torah	The Five Books of Moses; the first section of the Bible.
Zeman Matan Toratenu	The Time of the Giving of Our Torah, another name for Shavuot.

Learning Activities

Materials

A *Sefer Torah*; Bibles.

Opening

Ask the rabbi to show a *Sefer Torah* to students either in the classroom or in the sanctuary. If possible, unroll it on a table so that all the students can look at it at the same time.

Ask students what they know about the Torah. Ask: What is it? From what is it made? How is it written? What is in it? From where did it come? Feel free to correct or add to whatever is said. Then tell students that on Shavuot we celebrate the giving of the Torah and that this chapter will help them learn more about what is in the Torah.

Story Study (pp. 132-133)

1. Ask students the following questions:

   • This story is called a *midrash*, the name we give to a story that explains something that is not clear or not explained in the Torah. What question did the author of this story want to answer? (The question the author of this *midrash* wanted to answer was, Why did

God select the Children of Israel to receive the Torah and not some other nation?)

- According to this *midrash*, God calls the Israelites "My special people." What does being a special people mean? (According to this *midrash*, a special people is one that observes God's commandments.)

2. Read over the last paragraph of the story with students and ask them to explain why God selected Mount Sinai as the site to deliver the Torah.

Text Study Review (pp. 134-136)

1. Ask students the following questions:

- What does the word *Tanach* mean? (The Hebrew word *Tanach* refers to the entire Hebrew Bible, which consists of twenty-four books. Point out to students that the word *Tanach* is an acronym: The *tav* stands for Torah, the first five books of the Hebrew Bible; the *nun* stands for *Nevi'im*, Prophets; and the *chaf* stands for *Ketuvim*, Writings. *Nevi'im* and *Ketuvim* are made up of the remaining nineteen books of the Hebrew Bible.)

- What is *Tikun Leil Shavuot* and where did this custom originate? (*Tikun Leil Shavuot* is an all-night study session in which participants study verses from different parts of "the whole Torah"—the *Tanach* and the Talmud. The custom of studying the whole Torah in this manner originated in sixteenth-century Safed.)

- Which of the six passages from the Talmud do you find the most interesting? Why?

2. Divide the students into groups and give each group a Bible. Show students how to find Bible references. Have the groups practice using the Bible by asking them to find a series of passages.

3. Ask students to choose one of the *Tanach* texts from the mini-*tikun* in the textbook and find it in the Bible. Have them figure out the context of the quote by reading a few verses that precede it and a few verses that follow it. Ask students if what they've read changes or deepens their understanding of the passage quoted in the textbook.

4. Now ask students to choose a second *Tanach* text from the mini-*tikun*. Have them write a discussion question about that verse, one that you could then ask the rest of the class. Suggest to students that they once again look at the context of the quote in the Bible.

Holiday Experience Activities (pp. 137-139)

1. Have students close their book and try to list all the Ten Commandments without peeking. Tell them not to worry about listing the commandments in the right order.

2. Ask students to number the commandments in the order in which they

think the commandments *should* appear. Have students explain why they numbered the commandments the way they did. Afterward, have students compare the order in which they listed the commandments with the order in which the commandments appear on page 137 of the textbook.

3. Explain that the Ten Commandments can be grouped according to categories. For example, there are positive commandments and negative commandments. Have students suggest some other categories by which the commandments can be grouped. (Possible answers include: commandments that pertain to our relationship with God and those pertaining to our relationships with other people; commandments of the hand [deeds], the heart [beliefs], and the tongue [speech]; commandments with severe penalties, light penalties, and no penalties.)

4. Scholars debate whether the First Commandment is a commandment. Have students read it carefully (in Exodus 20:2 or on page 137 of the textbook) and then ask them the following questions:

    *   Do you think that it is a commandment? Why or why not?

    *   If you think that it is not, why do you suppose that it became one of the Ten Commandments?

5. Ask students the following questions:

    *   What problem did the Reform Jews of Germany try to solve by creating the ceremony of confirmation to replace the bar mitzvah ceremony? Do you think the solution worked? (The Reform Jews of Germany created the confirmation ceremony in order to extend the Jewish education of Jewish boys and girls who were attending public schools.)

    *   Why do you think Reform Jews chose Shavuot as the day on which to hold confirmation ceremonies? (Because the Jewish people received the Torah from God on Shavuot, it is fitting to hold a ceremony in which Jews acknowledge and embrace their Judaism as young adults on this holiday.)

    *   Do you think that bar/bat mitzvah and confirmation ceremonies serve an important purpose today? Why or why not? If you think that they do, what is that purpose?

6. Have students interview one or two confirmands who attend their synagogue or another synagogue. Suggest that students ask the confirmands about the confirmation customs and traditions that are followed at their synagogue. They could also ask the confirmands how they felt before, during, and after the ceremony. In addition, they might ask the confirmands whether they felt the experience was worthwhile and what they gained from it.

After students have completed their interview(s), have them report their findings to the class. Ask students how they feel about confirmation and whether they look forward to being confirmed.

Focus on Focus (p. 140)

1. Have students go to the library and explore in greater detail different views of revelation and what God said on Mount Sinai. Arrange for students to present a debate or talk show with different students espousing different points of view.

2. Ask students what they think happened at Mount Sinai.

Exploring Times and Places (pp. 141-142)

Ask students the following questions:

- Who was Ruth? Why do we read *Megillat Ruth* on Shavuot? (Ruth was one of Naomi's two Moabite daughters-in-law. We read the Book of Ruth because Ruth decided to accept the Torah and go to Israel, just as the Jewish people did.)

- Ruth's response to Naomi when Naomi urged her to return to her home is very famous: "Wherever you go, I shall go, and wherever you stay, I shall stay. Your people shall be my people, and your God, my God." Why are Ruth's words so significant? (Ruth's statement is remarkable for its bravery since Ruth could have chosen to return to her family and marry from among her own people.)

- What does "to glean in the fields" mean? From where does this custom come? (To glean means to gather grain or other produce left behind by reapers. This custom is derived from Leviticus 19:9–10, in which God commands the Jews to do the following: "When you reap the harvest of your land, you shall not reap all the way to the edges of your field, or gather the gleanings of your harvest. You shall not pick your vineyard bare, or gather the fallen fruit of your vineyard; you shall leave them for the poor and the stranger.")

Closure

Ask students what we celebrate on the festival of Shavuot. (the giving of the Torah) Tell students that although there are differing opinions about the Torah's origin, the Torah is the central text of Jewish tradition and that alone makes the Torah important.

Conclude this lesson by asking students why they think the Torah is important.

Enrichment Activity

It is customary to eat dairy foods and fruit on Shavuot. Here is a recipe for a typical Jewish dairy food.

Blintzes

Batter	*Filling*
3 eggs	2 cups cottage cheese, drained
1 cup milk	1 egg yolk
1/2 tsp. salt	1/2 tsp. salt
2 tbsps. oil	1 tbsp. butter
3/4 cup flour	2 tbsps. sugar
butter, margarine, or oil	1 tsp. lemon juice
	1/2 tsp. vanilla

Drain the liquid from the cottage cheese by placing it in a colander while the pancakes for the blintzes are being made. To make the batter, beat the eggs, milk, salt, and oil together. Stir in the flour. Heat some butter, margarine, or oil in a six-inch omelet pan. Pour about 2 tablespoons of the batter into the pan and tilt the pan so that the batter spreads to the edges. The goal is to make a very thin pancake. Cook the pancake until the bottom browns slightly. Place the pancake on a paper towel to remove any excess oil. Repeat the procedure with the rest of the batter.

Mix together all the ingredients for the filling. Take one pancake and place a heaping tablespoon of the filling in the center. Fold over the two ends of the pancake and then the two sides to enclose the filling. Repeat the procedure for all the pancakes. Fry the blintzes in a frying pan with a little butter, margarine, or oil until they are golden brown on both sides. Another option is to place the blintzes in a lightly oiled baking dish and bake in a 425° oven for 20 minutes or until they are golden brown. Serve with sour cream or applesauce.

Resources

Borowitz, Eugene. *Liberal Judaism.* New York: UAHC Press, 1984.

Borowitz, Eugene, and Naomi Patz. *Explaining Reform Judaism.* New York: Behrman House, Inc., 1985.

Diamant, Anita. *Living a Jewish Life.* New York: HarperCollins, 1991.

Chapter Fourteen

Tishah Be'av

Chapter Summary

- Tishah Be'av, the ninth day of the month of Av, is a day of mourning and fasting.

- On Tishah Be'av we remember the destruction of the First and Second Temples in Jerusalem.

- According to Jewish tradition and history, other tragic events also occurred on Tishah Be'av.

- On Tishah Be'av we read *Eichah*, the Book of Lamentations.

Instructional Objectives

Students will be able to:

- State why Rabbi Yohanan ben Zakkai is revered by Jews.

- Define the words *rebuke* and *consolation* and explain why we associate them with Tishah Be'av.

- Explain why some Jews choose not to observe Tishah Be'av.

Key Term

Eichah   The Book of Lamentations, one of the five
                                           megillot in the Bible.

Learning Activities

Materials

Dictionaries.

Opening

Ask students to list some of the things Jews do when we mourn for a person. Have students suggest some appropriate ways to mourn for the destruction of a city. Tell students that they will now learn about Tishah Be'av, a day on which we mourn for the destruction of the First and Second Temples and other tragic events in Jewish history.

Story Study (pp. 144-146)

Ask students the following questions:

- Who destroyed the First Temple? When? (The First Temple was destroyed in 586 B.C.E. by the Babylonians, who were led at that time by King Nebuchadnezzar.)

- Who destroyed the Second Temple? When? (The Second Temple was destroyed in 70 C.E. by the Romans, who were led by the Roman general and later emperor Vespasian.)

- Why do you think Jerusalem was so important to the conquerors? (Jerusalem and its surrounding area were important to the conquerors because several major military and trading routes crossed one another at that point.)

- How did Rabbi Yohanan ben Zakkai plan to save at least a few Jews? (At first, Rabbi Yohanan ben Zakkai tried to persuade the Jewish generals leading the rebellion to surrender Jerusalem. When this failed, he had his followers carry him out of the city in a white shroud, and he then approached Vespasian personally. After a series of verbal exchanges, Vespasian granted Rabbi Yohanan's request to establish an academy of Torah scholars in Yavneh.)

Text Study Review (p. 147)

Ask students the following questions:

- How can a city "become like a widow," as it says in Lamentations 1:1? What do you think the writer meant? (The writer of the Book of Lamentations uses a metaphor to convey the absence of the Jewish people from Jerusalem. The Jewish people are the husband who has died or been killed, leaving the city that was once a bride a widow.)

- How did the Jews feel when they saw the Babylonians conquering their beloved city? (The Book of Lamentations says that the people were miserable because of what had become of them and their home.

The writer probably expresses what all Jews were feeling when he writes, "My eye, my eye runs down with water, because the Comforter that should relieve my soul is far from me.")

- At the end of Lamentations 5:19-21, the writer says, "Return us to You, O *Adonai*.... Make us new, as in days of old!" What do you think the writer meant? How can something or someone be "new, as in days of old"? What did the Jews have in days of old that they now want back? (The writer asks God to make the Jews as they were when they first received the Torah and became a "new" people, ready to follow God's commandments and receive the promise and gift of the Land of Israel.)

Holiday Experience Activities (p. 148)

1. Have students look up the word *rebuke* in a dictionary and then ask them to give an example of a rebuke. Do the same with the word *consolation*.

2. Have students look at the two passages from Isaiah and then answer the following questions:

   - Whom is Isaiah rebuking? (Isaiah is rebuking the Israelites, ascribing their sufferings to their own sinfulness.)

   - What have the people done wrong? (According to Isaiah, the Israelites have turned against God by violating the commandments of the Torah and disobeying God's laws.)

   - What should the Israelites do to change their ways? (Isaiah tells his listeners that they must do good; look after the poor, the orphan, and the widow; seek justice; and do what is right.)

   - How does Isaiah console the people? (Isaiah tells the Israelites that their suffering is at an end and that the future holds the promise of reward and redemption.)

3. Ask students what the two passages on page 148 have to do with Tishah Be'av. Suggest that students look at a calendar and note when Tishah Be'av falls. Point out that Tishah Be'av comes before the High Holy Days. Ask students if they see a connection between Tishah Be'av and the High Holy Days. (Like the High Holy Days, Tishah Be'av is a time for us to recall our sins and suffering and to think about how we can make the world a better place in which to live.)

Focus on Focus (pp. 149-150)

1. Ask students to state the objections some Jews have raised concerning the observance of Tishah Be'av. (There are mainly two objections: In the early 1800s many Reform Jews began to feel that the great advances Jews had made in European countries rendered the observance of a holiday like Tishah Be'av superfluous. Others have argued that observing a

fast day in commemoration of Jerusalem's destruction seems unnecessary now that there is a Jewish state with Jerusalem as its capital.) Have students discuss what they think of these objections and whether they think the objections are valid or not.

2. It is true that Jews have suffered greatly at various times throughout history. Ask students if they think we need a day like Tishah Be'av to remind us about the tragic events in Jewish history. Have students explain their answer.

Something to Think About

1. Some parents complain that when Jewish history is taught in religious school, the focus is too often on the negative aspects of Jewish history. Ask students if they agree. Then have them discuss their view of Jewish history.

2. Although there have been many tragedies in Jewish history, many positive events have also occurred. Ask students what positive aspects of Jewish history and tradition they would include if they were designing a religious school curriculum. Have them explain why and how they would teach those aspects.

3. Ask students if they think Tishah Be'av belongs to the past. Then ask them if they think Jews of today should observe this fast. Have them explain their reasons.

Closure

Now that students have learned about all the holy days and festivals in the Jewish year, ask them to make a list of the Jewish holidays they have studied, along with a sentence or two about each one. Then have students work in pairs categorizing the holidays in as many different ways as possible. Suggest such categories as Biblical and Nonbiblical, Historical and Agricultural, Major and Minor, Happy and Sad, and so on. Tell students to keep in mind that some holidays will fit into more than one category. After students have completed this activity, have them compare their list with those of their classmates.